Sweden

120th anniversary
Berlitz

- A ☞ in the text denotes a highly recommended sight
- A complete A–Z of practical information starts on p.106
- Extensive mapping on cover flaps and throughout text

Berlitz Publishing Company, Inc.

Princeton   Mexico City   Dublin   Eschborn   Singapore

Original Text:	Doreen Taylor-Wilkie
Photography:	Bobby Andström
Editor:	Allison Laytin Greene
Layout:	Media Content Marketing, Inc.
Cartography:	GeoSystems Global Corporation
Cover Photo:	Courtesy of Sweden Travel and Tourism Council (Photographer: R. Ryan)

Although we make every effort to ensure the accuracy of all information in this book, changes do occur. If you find an error in this guide, please let our editors know by writing to us at Berlitz Publishing Company, 400 Alexander Park, Princeton, NJ 08540-6306. A postcard will do.

ISBN 2-8315-6995-8
Revised 1998 – First Printing September 1998

Printed in Switzerland
019/809 REV

CONTENTS

Sweden

SWEDEN AND
THE SWEDES

Sweden is the largest and most prosperous of the three Scandinavian countries (Sweden, Norway, and Denmark). This northern land is about the size of the American state of California, yet it is home to only 8.7 million people. With miles and miles of beautiful empty countryside, it is sometimes called the Green Lung of Europe. To fly over it is to soar across tracts of endless green land and countless lakes, from the huge surfaces of Vänern and Vättern—which are more like inland seas—to thousands of smaller waters that peer up like sparkling eyes out of the forests.

Even the three largest cities in Sweden, Stockholm, Gothenburg (the Swedes call it Göteborg), and Malmö, have their own open spaces, and sometimes it is hard to believe that you are in what is technically an "urban area."

Roughly 15 percent of the country lies beyond the Arctic Circle, and the farther north you travel the emptier the land becomes. To the east, the great river Torneälven hugs Sweden's border with Finland. If the character of a nation is shaped by the landscape in which its people have lived for generations, then this is the land that has done so much to make the Swedes what they are today.

Now in power since 1994, the Swedish Social Democratic party has suffered defeat in only two elections in the past 60 years. The most recent case was in 1991, when they lost heavily to a coalition of Moderate (led by Carl Bildt, who became Prime Minister), Liberal, Centre, and Christian Democrat parties.

At the time, a British interviewer remarked: "So, we're now seeing the end of the great Swedish welfare system?" The

Swedish commentator simply laughed. "You have to remember that this is only a change of emphasis," she replied, "We are not throwing out everything we've stood for overnight."

Such a remark goes a long way to summing up Swedes and the Swedish way of life. (If the same question had been asked in another land, it might have elicited an impassioned defence.) This is a consensus society which discusses *ad nauseum*; one of the most frustrating answers when you try to reach a Swede on the telephone is the apology: "Sorry, everyone's at a meeting."

That meeting could be about almost anything, from a business or organizational decision to whether the office bicycle park should have more spaces, or discussion of the current national issue — such as whether parents should be allowed to chastise their children physically (which is now forbidden) or whether to go ahead with the construction of a bridge between southern Sweden and Denmark (a debate that has dragged on for years, and has been resolved with construction of a tunnel-bridge link between Malanø and Copen-

Lilla Bommen, part of Gothenburg harbour, sends passengers and cargoes across the world.

hagen, to be completed in 2000). The essential thing is that everybody should have their say. On a larger scale, national or political issues are worked over in the same way, usually by a Commission, until an agreed view to which the majority of people can subscribe is absorbed into Swedish life.

At the root of this need for consensus is Sweden's closeness to its rural past, a life of small communities pulling together to survive the worst that nature could throw at them. It is hard to believe today, but only two or three generations ago, at the beginning of this century, Sweden's was still an impoverished rural society, with some 80 percent of the population scratching a living from the land.

Even then there were signs of the industrial success that was to follow. In barely one hundred years Sweden transformed itself into one of the world's richest countries, with a large number of people moving from outlying areas into the cities. Today, however sophisticated Swedish city-dwellers may seem, their ties to the land, though often subconscious, are nonetheless strong.

Only Norway and Denmark can equal the Swedish passion for getting out into *the* nature (*naturen*). This emphasis on the definite article stems not just from translation, but also from the importance Swedes attach to the outdoors and all things natural. Whether it's summer or winter, they just love to go walking, skiing, climbing, or, best of all, to immerse themselves in lake or sea.

Among the most popular pastimes are the late-summer expeditions into the forest to pick berries (something of a Swedish obsession), leaving a pleasing sensation that *the* nature has been used to good effect but has not suffered any damage. In the past, wild berries must have been a welcome addition to the diet. Today, the Swedes still use the traditional recipes but also serve berries in more sophisticated dishes

A Swedish musician in traditional garb strikes up a tune during festivities at Skansen.

—and store them in the deep freeze so that they can be enjoyed all year round.

A very telling symbol of the speed of change in Sweden, and of how much the Swedes still cherish their rural memories, is the success story of the open-air museum. It started at Skansen in Stockholm as long ago as 1891, when the far-sighted Artur Hazelius, realizing the rapidity with which the Industrial Revolution would transform Sweden, began to "collect" characteristic buildings, bringing them in timber by timber from different areas and reassembling them in natural groups.

Today, communities everywhere have similar collections where, at weekends and holidays, ordinary citizens as well as hired workers don traditional rural costumes and play at being old-time craftspeople, demonstrating age-old skills or dancing the traditional dances to familiar fiddle tunes.

If all this makes the Swedes sound somewhat earnest and serious (which is undoubtedly the impression they can give), it is not a true picture—and certainly not a complete one. As with any nation the Swedes have their own private humour, and the best jokes about Sweden and the Swedes are often told by the locals themselves. Once things get going, however, Swedish reticence fades fast. For proof, try a crayfish party marking the start of the crayfish season in August. As the aquavit circulates, the laughter and arguments get louder.

Few communities can celebrate old rural festivals with as much zest. In cities, towns, and villages, people light bonfires on Walpurgis night, welcoming spring after the dark days of winter; paint their children's faces for Easter; dance round the midsummer Maypole; eat *surströmming* (pungent, fermented herring); or revel in the lovely candlelit celebration of Lucia in December—all quite unselfconsciously, despite the Swedish reputation for reserve.

Externally, Swedes are not only taciturn but preserve a façade of satisfaction with all things Swedish—an attitude that often irks their Scandinavian neighbours. Such seeming arrogance, however, is no more than a hangover from the days of a rural, collective consciousness. Learn a little of the language and you'll be amazed at how critical of their government, political parties, modes, and methods Swedes can be as the evening wears on.

Every nation has its taboos, however, and Sweden's is alcohol. Possibly as a result of a once strong teetotal movement, the concept of "social drinking" (in the sense of going out for a quiet

Wild and forested Värmland, where Swedes get out into "the nature."

Sweden's many folk festivals provide occasion to smile.

drink) has never really taken off, though Friday and Saturday revelling is cheerful enough. Once the top is off a bottle it rarely goes back on again, and even the ferocious prices, notably of spirits, seem a scant deterrent to over-indulgence. Indeed, one popular answer to this problem is to distill your own. So, if you're offered a novel brand of aquavit in an obscure bottle, just lift your glass and say *skål* ("cheers").

Then again, the Swedish attitude to sex is very relaxed. Four out of seven partnerships are unwed and divorce is common: but the sense of family is still strong. The typical image is of a laden family car setting off on a Friday evening for the *stuga* (wooden house) next to the lake or forest. With the influx into the cities earlier this century, old farms and small wooden buildings in the countryside were abandoned. They are much in demand again, and if Swedes haven't inherited a *stuga,* they will build or buy one and spend as much time as possible—swimming, sailing, fishing, working on the house, or just enjoying the long summer evenings.

A BRIEF HISTORY

Pre-History, the Svear, and the Vikings

Mention Scandinavia and most people think of the Vikings, who swooped into the world arena around A.D. 800 in a fierce rush of longboats against an unguarded shore, killing and plundering as they went.

Such is the conventional view, but Scandinavia actually reaches back 12,000 years, to when the last Ice Age retreated. A basin of glacier and sea was left behind as huge subterranean convulsions forced the earth upwards. By 2000 B.C., the shape of the peninsula was much as it is today, and primitive hunters who had pushed north in the wake of the melting ice were now turning to farming and fishing.

During the Iron Age, independent tribes settled throughout the country, which came to be known as *Sverige,* or "Land of the Svear," after the tribe on the shores of Lake Mälaren. Traces of these early Swedes are found all around the lake.

The vast majority of the Swedish Vikings went east rather than west. Their reasons for sailing were complex indeed, but foremost in their minds were certainly thoughts of exploration, trade, and conquest. They

Decorated rune stones have long been a vital source of information about Viking times.

sailed deep into what is now Russia, spreading southeast as far as Constantinople, where some joined the Imperial Guard. An Arab historian described them as "great mustachioed angels, of evil disposition and smell."

Much information about the early Svear has come to light through excavations at Birka, Sweden's first town (see page 34). At its height (in A.D. 800–975), Birka was the trading centre for a lakeside population of some 40,000 people, and now many graves and archaeological remains are dotted around Mälaren's shores. The Vikings are also recalled in tall rune stones decorated with a script that has long been decipherable. These are mostly around Lake Mälaren, Skåne, and the islands of Gotland and Öland, but one has been found as far north as Östersjön in Jämtland.

The Middle Ages

Christianity did not so much march into Sweden as slip in cautiously. In the ninth century the Frankish monk St. Ansgar was allowed to preach to the people of Birka (see page 34), and around A.D. 1000, Olof Skötkonung, the first Christian king of the Swedes, was baptized into the Byzantine Church (he had close ties with Constantinople). His sons Anund Jakob and Edmund supported Christianity, too, but did not succeed in bringing the Swedes to the new religion, and ended by ruling only the area of Västergötland in the southwest.

In the mid-12th century, the pretender king Erik Jedvardsson (Erik IX, later St. Erik, patron saint of the Swedes) was converted to Christianity, but only hesitantly did the Swedes give up the fierce paganism instilled by the Vikings.

Another strong medieval influence on Sweden was the German trading society (the Hanseatic League, or Hansa), which at that time controlled trade in most of northern Europe. The Hansa was well rooted in Sweden, particularly

Historical Landmarks

c. A.D. 94	Roman historian Tacitus mentions *Svear*.
8th–11th century	Swedish Vikings range through Russia as far as Constantinople.
829–831	Ansgar tries to introduce Christianity.
993–1024	Reign of Olof Skötkonung, first Christian king of Sweden.
1150–1160	Erik Jedvardsson is baptized, spreads Christianity, and captures Finland (1157).
12th century	Hanseatic League begins to dominate trade.
1397	Denmark, Sweden, and Norway united.
1435	Meeting of the first Riksdag (Parliament).
1520	Stockholm Bloodbath.
1523	Gustav Vasa elected king; founds the Swedish nation state and the Vasa dynasty.
1527	Gustav Vasa imposes Reformation.
1611–1632	Reign of Gustav II Adolf.
1718	Karl XII killed and Vasa dynasty ends.
1718–1771	Age of Freedom; Riksdag gains in power.
18th century	Gustav III promotes culture and arts.
1808–1809	Sweden loses Finland to Russia.
1810	French marshal Jean-Baptiste Bernadotte becomes Crown Prince.
1814	Danes cede Norway to Sweden.
1818	Crown Prince becomes King Karl XIV Johan of Sweden-Norway.
1880s–1890s	Industrial Revolution begins. Agricultural crisis leads to mass Swedish emigration.
1905	Norway gains independence.
1914–1918	World War I; Sweden remains neutral.
1932	Social Democrats elected.
1939–1945	World War II; Sweden declares neutrality.
1991	Elections won by non-Socialist coalition.
1995	Sweden joins European Union.
1998	Stockholm selected as cultural capital of Europe.

on the island of Gotland, and enjoyed good trade between the Baltic and Germany.

In the 13th century, Sweden was taking control of what later became Finland, and there were alternating periods of harmony and strife with Denmark. In 1397, Denmark, under the rule of forceful Queen Margareta, united the three countries by way of the Kalmar Union.

Alhough Denmark and Norway were to remain united until 1814, Sweden's membership did not last much longer than a stormy century. The country withdrew in 1523, with the accession to the Swedish throne of Gustavus I (Gustav Vasa).

The Kalmar Union brought to the fore Swedish men such as Engelbrekt Engelbrektsson, a minor noble who led a rebellion against Danish taxes in 1434, as well as Sten Sture, who changed Swedish history by defeating the Danish King Christian I at the Battle of Brunkeberg in 1471.

During its last 50 years, the Kalmar Union was anything but united, ending with the infamous Stockholm Bloodbath of 1520, when the Danish King Christian II held a feast for many of Sweden's greatest citizens, then executed 82 of them in Stockholm's Stortorget (see page 43).

The Royal Dynasties

From the early 15th century until the beginning of the 20th century, Sweden's history can be neatly divided into periods under different royal houses.

Gustav Vasa was in exile in Denmark when his father, two uncles, and a brother-in-law were killed in the Stockholm Bloodbath. He hurried home to raise the country to arms and, once Sweden was freed, was elected king on 6 June 1523 (celebrated throughout Sweden now as National Day).

Vasa was a superb administrator and politician as well as a warrior. He harnessed the Hansa and reduced its power, cleverly manoeuvred the warring nobles and rich farmers, suppressed uprisings, and in 1527 implemented the Reformation, seizing control of the Church's lands and breaking its power and wealth over the next 15 years. (The first Swedish Bible appeared in 1541.) His aim was less religious than financial, for like King Henry VIII of England, he found the Church's riches extremely useful. (Monuments built by Gustav Vasa include the fortress-palaces at Vadstena, Uppsala, and Gripsholm.)

His grandson, Gustav II Adolf, proved to be yet another brilliant warrior-statesman. During the Thirty Years' War, he crossed over the Baltic so successfully against Livonia (Estonia and Latvia), Russia, and Poland that it became known as "the Swedish Pond." At home, he left affairs in the capable hands of his excellent Chancellor, Axel Oxenstierna, who owned Tidö Slott on Lake Mälaren's south side (see page 39).

King Gustav II Adolf was one of Sweden's greatest military geniuses, and might have brought even more changes to the map of Europe, had he not been killed during the Thirty Years' War. He died at the age of 38 at the Battle of Lützen in 1632, in which Sweden beat the forces of the Holy Roman Empire. Like Gustav Vasa, he did much to open up Sweden, creating new towns, many in the

This statue at Mora in Dalarna is one of many commemorating the great Gustav Vasa.

north, such as Umeå and Luleå (see pages 75 and 76), and his greatest memorial, Gothenburg (see page 54).

King Gustav II Adolf was succeeded by his daughter, Kristina, then still a child, who abdicated in 1654 in favour of her cousin, Karl X. With him the Vasa dynasty's military genius flared again, albeit briefly, when he attacked Denmark in 1658 in a daring raid over the ice, forcing the Danes to hand over what are now Skåne, Halland, Blekinge, and Gotland.

In 1697, the boy-king Karl XII inherited a strong kingdom with many overseas possessions, but also a legacy of war. Indeed, the Swedes look on Karl XII as a romantic military hero. In reality, however, after storming across Europe successfully, his army was very nearly wiped out by the Rus-

---

Queen Kristina

The warrior king, Gustav II Adolf, raised his daughter Kristina as he would have a son. One commentator was to write: "Science is to Kristina what needle and cotton are to other women." She was only six when her father died at Lützen, and inherited the throne with the advantage of Gustav's formidable Chancellor, Axel Oxenstierna, as Regent.

Around the age of 16 Kristina began to attend her Council's meetings, and by the time she became queen in 1644 she well understood the ways of government. She presided over a sumptuous Baroque court filled with brilliant young minds that could match hers in knowledge and wit, but later grew bored with her role as queen and quarrelled with her Chancellor. One possible reason for her abdication in 1654 was her increasing sympathy with the Roman Catholic faith, coupled with her reluctance to marry. She travelled to Rome, where she shocked her former subjects by announcing her conversion. Her response was: "Men can never admire, never approve a deed which they themselves are incapable of performing."

sians under Peter the Great in 1709 at the Battle of Poltava in the Ukraine. The 50,000-strong Russian army slaughtered the 20,000 Swedes, leaving only 1,500 to flee south to Turkey with the king. Karl spent five years in Turkey and then, in a 15-day endurance test, rode for 2,100 km (1,300 miles) across Europe to return to Scandinavia. He was killed while fighting the Norwegians at Fredriksten fortress in Norway, just over the border from Bohuslän (see page 59) in 1718. He had not set foot in his capital city in 18 years, and his death ended not only the Vasa dynasty but Sweden's era as a great European power.

Freedom and Enlightenment

This was the beginning, however, of a great age of freedom, with the transfer of power from the monarch to the Riksdag (parliament). A Swedish talent for invention also began to emerge at this time, eventually leading to the practical industrial developments of the late 19th and early 20th centuries. Botanist Carl von Linné (Linneaus, 1707–1778) published his definitive system for classifying plants, astronomer Anders Celsius (1701–1744) invented the 100-degree thermometer, and there were several successful chemists, including C.W. Scheele (1742–1786), who was the first to analyse the components of air as oxygen and nitrogen.

Liberty did not last long. Proud of being the first Swedish-born king since Karl XII, Gustav III ascended the throne in 1771 and moved steadily towards absolutism and autocratic rule. His most significant achievement was to found a native Swedish culture—indeed, his rule fell within the wider period known as the Gustavian Enlightenment. He ordered the building of Stockholm's Royal Opera House and Royal Dramatic Theatre, and transformed the theatre at Drottningholm Court into a showcase for Swedish talent.

King Gustav III was a fine writer himself, and attracted men of letters to the Court, encouraging them by founding the Swedish Academies of Literature, Music, Art, and History and Antiquities. For all his preoccupation with the arts and culture, however, the king could not ignore the wars with Russia that grumbled on periodically right up to the 19th century. Nor could his increasing autocracy fail to disturb the old noble families, who felt their power slipping away to Gustav's more pliable favourites. The nobles plotted, with the result that Gustav's death could have been part of one of the operas he loved. He was assassinated at a masked opera ball—an event that was to inspire Verdi's opera *Un Ballo in Maschera*.

The Making of Modern Sweden

As the Gustavian era faded away in rivalry and muddle, in 1808 Sweden lost Finland to Russia after a fierce two-year war. The first decade of the 19th century was marked by several great changes in agriculture, constitution, foreign policy

Sweden's renowned botanist, Carl von Linné, is remembered at his museum in Uppsala.

and, most noticeably at the time, dynasty. In 1810 the Riksdag, now with a written Constitution, invited a French marshal in Napoleon's army, Jean-Baptiste Bernadotte, to become Crown Prince. It was a strange choice, particularly since Bernadotte had at one time headed an army waiting in Denmark to invade Sweden, but one that proved justified. A firm hand was needed and the Swedes—who did not have confidence in Frederik VI of Denmark, the other main candidate for the position—found Bernadotte resolute in tackling the aftermath of the years of internal unrest.

Sweden's long struggle with Russia came to an end in 1809, with the surrendering of Finland to Czar Alexander. Sweden then devoted the second half of the 19th century to internal development; a late industrial revolution, using its natural assets in mining, saw-milling, and the manufacturing of wood-pulp; and promoting its successes in the inventive field, such as Alfred Nobel's dynamite and Gustav Pasch's safety match (see page 62). There was progress with the arrival of the co-operative movement, trade unionism, and stirrings of the social democratic and women's movements.

Political problems nevertheless still demanded attention. In 1814 the Danes had handed Norway to Sweden, but the Norwegians objected and set up their own independent parliament. As a compromise, in 1818 the Crown Prince was crowned King Karl XIV Johan of Sweden-Norway. He was wise enough to rule gently, but a growing sense of national identity and a cultural renaissance led Norway along the road to statehood. Friction increased between the two countries until, in 1905, the union between Sweden and Norway came to an end.

In addition, a mounting agricultural crisis in the 1880s led to the emigration of what was eventually to be a total of more than one million people by the 1930s. So many Swedes settled in North America that some communities in Minnesota and Wisconsin subsequently spoke only Swedish for at least one generation. Today, thousands of these pioneers' descendants return to Sweden to visit their roots every year.

The 20th Century

Despite the successes of the 19th century—including the establishment of a railway network, universal education, and a good supply of raw materials—Sweden entered the 20th century a poor country, with 80 percent of the population involved in farming or rural industries. The Industrial Revolution brought poverty at first, but industrialization took hold rapidly, so that during World War I the demand for Swedish products reached a premium, bringing new-found hope.

No sooner were things picking up than the Great Depression that swept across most of the industrial world hit Sweden. The country was plagued by widespread bouts of unemployment. Strikes took place, leading to a tragic incident in 1931 in which soldiers opened fire on several thousand demonstrators from Ångermanland, injuring many and killing five, including a woman bystander.

Political changes happened gradually, without bloodshed; the introduction of universal suffrage in 1921 led to a system of elections, political parties, and a democratic government.

In the early years of the 1900s, the monarchy found itself under pressure with calls for the abdication of Gustav V. The king rode the storm, however, and emerged as a popular ruler after World War I. His great-grandson, the present King, Carl XVI Gustav, has done much to ensure the monarchy's well-being.

This century has also been a period of social democracy and national neutrality, with Sweden refusing to take part in either World War, though the country has since been active in the United Nations. The Social Democrats have been in power for most of the last 70 years—even during periods of govern-

*Mounted police at Riksdagshuset (Swedish parliament),
in Stockholm's Old Town.*

ments of Moderates, Liberals, and Centre parties, the differences between left and right have not been split across the chasm of opposing ideologies found in many other countries.

Even the most dramatic and tragic recent event, the still-unexplained assassination of the Social Democratic Prime Minister, Olof Palme, in 1986, did not lead to further bloodshed and instability. His death shook the nation's confidence; the international furor that followed indicated his stature as a world statesman. In the 1980s Sweden suffered an economic downswing, from which the country is now recovering. There has been a general unraveling of some of the socialist underpinnings of the economy.

Through its involvement with the United Nations and other organizations, Sweden plays a role far beyond its own borders, particularly with the establishment by businesses of links and satellite companies all over the world.

In November 1994 a national referendum on membership to the European Union resulted in a slim majority for those in favour. On 1 January 1995, Sweden officially joined the EU.

WHERE TO GO

Sweden is the fourth largest country in Europe. Across 75 percent of the land, the population density is only six people per km^2 (15 per square mile), so there are long stretches between towns. It's better not to attempt to tackle the whole country in one visit.

We have divided Sweden into five main regions, each of which is subdivided according to old provincial names. These may not coincide with local government regions, but they are the names used by the Swedes themselves.

STOCKHOLM

From any one of Stockholm's bridges, it is easy to see that the Swedish capital is a city of sea and lake. Lake Mälaren in the west gives way to Saltsjön, the start of the Baltic Sea, in the east, and everywhere trees, gardens, and buildings of mellow red stone and modern glass are never far from water.

The city covers 14 islands. At a time when water provided the easiest transport route, the small settlement where sea met lake quickly became the gateway to inland Sweden. Today, salt and freshwater are divided by the heavy lock gates of Slussen. Big Baltic ferries wait at the quays, and, in summer, boats with bright sails scurry over the sparkling surface. Perhaps the most remarkable thing is that these waters are as clean as they look. Indeed, there are few capitals in the world where you can swim and fish for salmon right in the city centre.

The heart of the city is very compact, and best covered either on foot, or, as an introduction, by sight-seeing boat from Stadhuskajen. The main areas are Gamla Stan (Old Town); Norrmalm, the modern business centre; Östermalm, an up-market residential suburb, Djurgården, Stockholm's outdoor play-

Sweden Highlights

Stockholm and Surroundings

Drottningholm Court Theatre, Royal Palace Grounds on Lovön in Lake Mälaren. By boat from Stadshuskajen. (See page 33)

Djurgården, Stockholmers' outdoor playground, with Skansen open-air museum. By boat from Slussen. (See page 30)

Hammarby, home of Carl von Linné (Linneaus), with a fine botanical garden. South of Uppsala. May–Sept. (See page 36)

The South

Bosjökloster, with a 12th-century church and *Ringsjön* bird lake. April–Oct 8am–8pm; at Höör, near Lund, Skåne. (See page 41)

Utvandrarnas hus, at Växjö, the largest European archive on emigration; tel. (0) 470-475-75 for opening times. (See page 50)

Gothenburg and the West

Trädgårdsföreningen. Glorious gardens, palm and butterfly houses, children's theatre—much more than a park. (See page 58)

Tanum's Bronze Age Carvings, best seen in the evening; tours run by *Vitlycke Hällristningsmuseum*; tel. (0) 525-209-50. (See page 59)

Håverud Aqueduct. Great 19th-century engineering feat on the Dalsland Canal, near the Håfreströmmen rapids. (See page 60)

The Central Heartlands

Midsummer celebrations at Rättvik and "church-boats" on Lake Siljan. (See page 64)

Frösön Island, where the Viking drama/opera, *Arnljot*, is played out-of-doors in July. (See page 72)

Wild Bears at Sånfjället National Park. South of highway 84, northwest of Sveg in Härjedalen; tel. (0) 63-14-60-00. (See page 70)

Norrland and the Arctic

Midnight Sun over Lake Torneträsk. The unique phenomenon seen at its best. North of Kiruna on E10 to Abisko. (See page 81)

Ájtte. Excellent museum in Jokkmokk offers a vivid portrayal of the Sami world and the 18th- and 19th-century settlers. (See page 80)

Arctic Hall. World's biggest igloo built each winter at Jukkasjärvi, 15 km (10 miles) from Kiruna. (See page 82)

ground; and Södermalm, literally the "southern section." Pleasant suburbs stretch along the water to the west and east, housing a significant portion of Greater Stockholm's population of around 1.6 million (only 700,000 live in the city itself). Beyond the suburbs are the alluring islands of Lake Mälaren to the west and the 24,000 islands of the *skärgård* (archipelago) to the east.

Gamla Stan

Take a stroll down one of the history-laden cobbled streets of Gamla Stan.

What better place to start than Gamla Stan (Old Town), where Stockholm itself began its history more than seven centuries ago? Cross by the Riksbron (bridge) and your route will take you literally through the Swedish **Riksdagshuset** (the Parliament building), with its new wing glinting in the sun. Some time ago excavations revealed part of a medieval city here, below the Riksdag terrace. Part of the area has been turned into the **Medeltidsmuseet** (Medieval Museum), with the old wall and town gallows *in situ*.

Just beyond the Riksdag is **Kungliga Slottet** (the Royal Palace), with 608 rooms (one more, they say, than Buckingham Palace). The present building was built on the site of Tre Kronor (Three Crowns) Palace, which was designed and started by Nicodemus Tessin, the Swedish royal architect, in 1646–1681, continued by his son and grandson, and then razed by fire in 1697. A visit here requires time, since the palace (now no longer the royal family's main residence) houses no less than five separate museums and is famous for its Gobelin and Swedish tapestries.

Below the main building is the **Royal Armoury,** with the stuffed horse and armour of the renowned warrior king, Gustav II Adolf. Also below ground are the **Crown Jewels,** beautifully lit and displayed in the **Skattkammaren** (Royal Treasury). The Apartments of State and other rooms with magnificent interiors are open to the public, including **Oskar II's Writing Room,** full of 19th-century furniture and unaltered since the king's death in 1907. Each day in summer the Royal Guard parades gravely down Norrmalm's Hamngatan, and over the bridge to the palace for the Changing of the Guard at noon (1:00 P.M. Sunday).

Right next to the palace is the **Storkyrkan** (Cathedral), a high-ceilinged Gothic building and Stockholm's oldest, dating from around 1250. Used as a parish church and for ceremonial occasions, it holds the famous statue of **St. George and the Dragon,** a large woodcarving by Bernt Notke from 1489. The nearby **Tyska Kyrkan,** the German Church, is almost as old, a reminder of the medieval German traders. Every

An aerial view of Gamla Stan and the waters of Stockholm beyond.

four hours the bells of Tyska Kyrkan echo over Gamla Stan in two alternating hymn melodies.

At any time, people throng the shopping streets of Västerlånggatan and Österlånggatan. This is the area to wander, and to visit **Mårten Trotzigs Gränd,** the narrowest street of all, at the southern end of Västerlånggatan; more a stairway than a lane, it is less than one metre (3 feet) wide.

At the centre of this tangle of streets is **Stortorget,** the square in which 82 Swedes were killed in the Stockholm Bloodbath (see page 16). During the Christmas period, a market is held here every day. On one side is **Börsen** (Stock Exchange), where each year in an upstairs room the Swedish Academy picks the winner of the Nobel Prize for Literature.

Over a bridge to the west is **Riddarholmen** (Island of the Nobles), with the distinctive lattice-work spire of the 700-year-old **Riddarholmskyrkan** (Church of the Nobility),

The spire of Riddarholmskyrkan has towered over Riddarholmen for some 700 years.

where all the nation's monarchs since Gustav II Adolf are entombed in fine sarcophagi.

Norrmalm

Norrmalm is the capital city's commercial, banking, and business centre, with many hotels and restaurants, and famous stores such as NK and Åhléns (see page 84). Also here are the **Royal Opera House,** with its well-known Operakällaren restaurant and Café Operan (see page 142), and the **Kungliga Dramatiska Teatern,** where Max von Sydow and Greta Garbo, among others, made appearances early in their careers.

Although many older buildings survived the construction boom of the 1960s, some were replaced by modern blocks, and Norrmalm became all the poorer for it. The demolition process was stopped, however, when the Stockholmers rebelled and climbed the trees in **Kungsträdgården,** a pleasant square off Hamngatan, defying the men who had come to bulldoze the area. Thanks to them, Kungsträdgården remains the open-air heart of Norrmalm, with trees, flowers, games, and small galleries. On one side, **Sverigehuset** (Sweden House) has a **tourist information office** and booking centre for excursions (see page 123).

A memorial to the period of demolition is **Sergels Torg,** a huge square with a giant glass obelisk at the top of Hamngatan. Opposite is the **Kulturhuset,** a modern arts centre and meeting place, while below the square is a lower level of walkways and covered shopping arcades, such as the **Gallerian,** which are ideal in winter.

For a taste of one of Stockholm's popular street markets, stroll along Sergelgatan past the glass skyscrapers to **Hötorget,** a typical, colourful fruit, flower, and vegetable market. Here, too, is the **Konserthuset,** base of the Stockholm Philharmonic Orchestra and a venue for a variety of concerts, from classical

Kungliga Slottet (the Royal Palace) houses no less than five museums.

to rock. In front of this fine building stands the lovely **Orpheus Fountain,** the work of Carl Milles, one of Sweden's most famous sculptors (see page 34).

To the west, Norrmalm ends at Tegelbacken, with a good view of the **Stadshuset** (City Hall) on the next island of Kungsholmen. From any point in the south of the city it is hard to miss its massive square tower, 105 metres (450 feet) high and topped with the golden Tre Kronor (three crowns) that are the city's symbol. Boats for Mälaren (see page 33) depart from the quay below.

Inside, the Golden Hall, venue for the glittering Nobel Dance, is all marble and gilded mosaics, while the Blue Hall, with its great staircase inspired by the Doges' Palace in Venice, is the scene of the Nobel Dinner.

☛ Djurgården

Djurgården ("deer park") was once a royal hunting ground and has retained much of its rural feel. From Nybroplan, at the base of Hamngatan, you can reach the island on foot or by bus. The route passes through adjacent Östermalm, where fine old buildings line the Strandvägen waterside.

In summer, it is romantic to take the ferry from Slussen, which gives you a chance to see the harbour and the myriad small boats that sail out to the archipelago each weekend.

The short ferry trip takes you past a graceful boat, the *Af Chapman* (now a youth hostel), and the fortress island of Kastellholmen.

Skeppsholmen, just behind Kastellholmen, is the permanent home for the **Moderna Museet** (Museum of Modern Art). The museum, reopened in 1998 after extensive refurbishment, houses a collection that includes works by Picasso, Dali, Kandinsky, and other international and Swedish artists. Near its Skeppsholmen site is the **Östasiatiska Museet** (Museum of Asian Art), with exhibitions that include a fine collection of Chinese art once belonging to King Gustav VI Adolf.

The northernmost of the islands (all linked by bridges) is Blasieholmen, more a peninsula than the other two. Here you'll find the **Nationalmuseum** (National Museum of Art), with works by 16th- to 19th-century European masters and by the great Swedish painters Anders Zorn and Carl Larsson.

As the ferry nears Djurgården, the thrills and spills of the rides at **Gröna Lund,** a 19th-century amusement park, loom

---

Breaking the Language Barrier

Getting to grips with the Swedish language can take time. The following list of common words should be useful.

älv/ån	river	*öst*	east
berg, fjäll	mountain	*sjö/träsk*	lake
bro	bridge	*slott/hus*	castle
gata	street	*söder*	south
gränd	lane	*stad*	town
hamn	harbour, port	*strand*	beach
kyrka	church	*torg, plan, plats*	square
museet	the museum	*trädgården*	garden
nord	north	*väg/vägen*	road
ö or holme	island	*väst*	west

Moderna Museet—recently reopened after renovations— houses an extensive collection of modern art.

into view, among them the stomach-churning scenic railway and a traditional Ferris wheel. For the more discerning visitor, however, Djurgården means the Vasa Museum and Skansen.

The **Vasa warship** was built as the pride of the fleet for Gustav II Adolf, but, unfortunately, pride did indeed come before a fall. Top-heavy from the weight of her guns and decoration, the Vasa sank on her maiden voyage, drowning many on board before the eyes of the horrified monarch and the many Stockholmers who were there for the occasion.

She was discovered in the 1950s by a determined marine archaeologist, Anders Franzén, who salvaged her in 1961. Piecemeal restoration over 30 years has returned her to excellent condition and now, in a new museum, the Vasa is a magnificent sight, with several "cutaway" floors that reveal the structure from keel to decks.

Skansen, on the other hand, is out-of-doors, a re-created village where craftspeople display traditional skills. It is a place in which to linger and perhaps sample old sweets: try the delicious *bullar*, traditional and popular spicy buns.

This island playground also boasts two good museums. The **Nordiska Museet** (Nordic Museum) explains Nordic life from the 16th century on, with many specialized exhibitions, while the **Biologiska Museet** shows Nordic animals against dioramas to give the impression of a natural habitat.

There are various galleries here too, including the **Thielska Galleriet,** once the collection of a Stockholm banker, and the delightful **Waldemarsudde,** former home of the so-called "painter prince" Eugén, brother to Gustav V. This exquisite gallery, with particularly fine gardens, holds the Prince's whole collection—generally Nordic paintings from 1880 to 1940 and including several landscapes painted by his own hand.

Lake Mälaren and the Archipelago

Lake Mälaren stretches 100 km (62 miles) west of Stockholm and has innumerable enticing islands. A good day out is by vintage steamer to Drottningholm on Lovön (some 50 minutes from Stadshuskajen).

Lovön has long been a royal island. **Drottningholm Palace,** built in the 17th century and now the royal family's main home, has a wonderful garden, a smaller version of Versailles. A large portion of the palace is open to the public. Most popular is **Drottningholm Court Theatre,** built in 1766 by Queen Louisa Ulrika, the mother of Sweden's great patron of the arts, Gustav III. He encouraged theatre and arts of every variety and his reign became a Golden Age. The graceful little theatre flourished and served to entertain the Royal Court, which also amused itself in both the **Kina Slott** (Chinese Palace) and its grounds nearby.

All this ended when Gustav III was assassinated, fittingly, at a masked ball. The Court Theatre was shut and forgotten until the 1920s, when Professor Agne Beijer pushed open the door and, to his astonishment, found the 18th-century theatre, perfectly preserved.

Opera and ballet are performed here in the summer, or you can accompany daily guided tours of the theatre, complete with original backdrops and 18th-century equipment. If you're at a performance, note the court officials' names, which are still discernible on the seat backs. (Tickets are sold at the kiosk on Norrmalmstorg, which will also provide details of events at many Stockholm venues.)

Farther west is the island of **Björkö,** with the remains of Sweden's oldest settlement, the Viking town of **Birka.** Archaeological digs have shown that from A.D. 800 to 975 Birka was a trading centre of 40,000 people on the shores of Lake Mälaren. In those days, nothing divided the lake from the Baltic Sea, and travellers sailed in from Russia and Arabia. It was then that St. Ansgar, a Frankish monk, arrived from Europe to convert the local tribes (see page 14). The chapel on Björkö, built in the 1930s, is dedicated to him.

East of the city centre are the inner islands of the archipelago, which are best seen on an excursion that lasts about seven hours. In summer, water sets the mood for **Millesgården,** the summer home of sculptor Carl Milles (1875–1955), on **Lidingö.** Here he reproduced the statues that had made him famous. Set on steep terraces, the figures seem to fly, almost defying gravity.

Although close to the city, the **Fjäderholmarna** (Feather Islands) form a genuine archipelago. These rocky, tree-cov-

Sigtuna—located off the E4 route from Stockholm to Uppsala—is worth a visit for its ruined monasteries.

ered islets have an aquarium of Baltic fish, a smoke-house, and an archipelago museum.

Vaxholm is a great place for watersports. The **Fortress** at Vaxholm dates from the 16th century and was built to guard Stockholm's main sea route. Vaxholm now has more peaceful purposes—its attractions include the **Homestead Museum,** housed in a fishing cottage, and the old **Customs House,** and the fortress is also the setting for special "Herring Picnics" (included in some of the tours).

Two or three hours into the Baltic, **Sandhamn** on **Sandön** is a well-known summer haunt; a village with sandy beaches. Seafarers from many lands rest peacefully in its cemetery, and the **Sandhamns Värdshus** restaurant has been feeding sailors ever since 1672.

STOCKHOLM'S SURROUNDINGS

Uppsala

Stockholm sits south of Uppland, on the border between Södermanland and Uppland. This area includes the old capital
of **Uppsala,** which saw the last days of heathen Sweden.

Today, Uppsala is the seat of Sweden's Archbishop and can
boast Scandinavia's largest **Gothic Cathedral.** Here, too, is
Sweden's oldest university, which ensures a lively student con-
tingent around the narrow streets. Students once gathered in the
Anatomical Theatre to watch operations being performed.

Famous alumni of the university include Carl von Linné
(Linnaeus), botanist, and Dag Hammarskjöld, a great poet,
peacemaker, and former Secretary General of the United Nations. Carl von Linné's legacy is the **Linnéträdgården** (Linné Gardens), a beautiful oasis of plants. His summer home,
Hammarby, has a small but fine botanic garden.

The city is dominated by its **Castle,** a brick fortress where
Gustav II Adolf held talks that plunged Sweden into the Thirty Years' War, and where Queen Kristina gave up her crown.

Off the E4 route to Uppsala from Stockholm are the ruined
monasteries of **Sigtuna,** while farther north, in a cluster of
lakes, you will find **Skokloster,** the seat of the Wrangles, an
important family that once ruled much of Scandinavia. Today
their great white house, with a large collection of 17th-centu-
ry weapons and a motor museum, is open to the public.

Around the Lake

Leaving Stockholm on the E20/E4 on Mälaren's southern
side, the first stop is the idyllic small town of **Mariefred**—
which can also be reached by steamship from Stadhuskajen.
This is a typical lakeside town with 16th-century **Gripsholm**

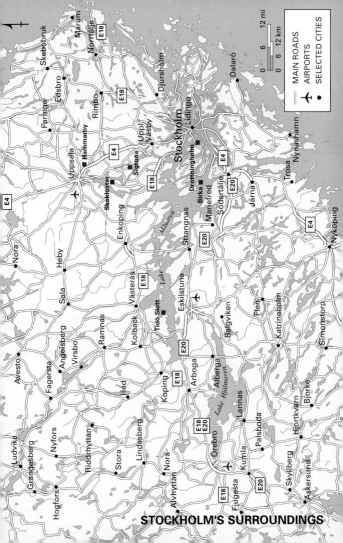

STOCKHOLM'S SURROUNDINGS

The idyllic fields of Mariefred, a small town that can be reached by rail or steamship.

Slott, once owned by Gustav Vasa. Gripsholm's royal portraits are quite compelling, and a small theatre goes back to the days of that royal patron of the arts, Gustav III. Another delight is the **Östra Södermanlands Järnväg** (the East Södermanland Railway), a superb steam railway between Mariefred and Läggesta, 4 km (2½ miles) away.

West from Gripsholm, 17th-century **Sundbyholm** has been turned into a hotel and restaurant, from where **Sigurdsristningen,** an ancient rock carving, is a short walk through the beech woods.

Eskilstuna recalls the great days of steel and iron, and the **Rademacher Smithies,** founded in 1658, are now an industrial museum. The city also has a popular zoo park with a pride of white tigers.

From Eskilstuna retrace the road back to the pretty little town of **Strängnäs** to see the vast **Gothic Cathedral.** From here, head north by route 55 over bridges and islands to Lake Mälaren's northern bank. A side road west leads to the ancient estate of **Ängsö Slott,** full of old legends, on its own island of **Ängsö**—a good place for swimming, fishing, canoeing, and walking; you'll also find a pleasant campsite here.

Heading west on the E18 you come to **Västerås,** an early trade centre, with a **Cathedral** that holds the tomb of Erik XIV. Not far away, **Anundshög** has Sweden's largest Iron Age burial mounds and ship tumuli. Västerås is also a pleasure-sailing centre linked to the capital by ferry.

South of Västerås, the 17th-century **Tidö Slott** was the home of Axel Oxenstierna, the great Swedish Regent who ruled during the minority of Gustav II's daughter, Kristina. Today, Tidö houses a **Toy Museum** with some 35,000 items, and the grounds are home to hundreds of deer.

Close to the western end of Lake Mälaren is another castle, **Strömsholm Slott,** which was once a royal residence. There is an excellent riding centre with a carriage museum here. Watersports enthusiasts should head towards **Kolbäcksån** and, close by, the **Strömsholm Canal.** At the end of the lake, where the road joins the E20 from the south side, **Arboga** has some of the best preserved buildings in Sweden. In 1435 this town was the meeting place for what later became Sweden's first Riksdag (parliament) and for the election of Engelbrekt Engelbrektsson to the position of Captain of the Realm (see page 16).

West, the land rises into the mountainous area of Bergslagen, where the birthplace of Swedish steel, **Örebro,** sits at the western end of Lake Hjälmaren. Örebro, the main town of Sweden's smallest province, Närke, also has a fine castle. Two places recall mining days: **Lilla Nora,** wooden houses form a well-preserved 19th-century village where the steel workers lived long ago; and **Siggebohyttan**'s manor house illustrates the luxury in which the rich mill-owners once lived.

THE SMILING SOUTH

The south of Sweden between the Kattegat and the Baltic has a character shaped by both history and proximity to Continental Europe. It is also mellowed by a warmer climate and made more cosmopolitan by its role as a summer playground.

Skåne

Thanks to its fertility, Skåne is known as "Sweden's Granary." The province is somehow different from the rest of Sweden; even the accent has a hint of Danish—no surprise, as it's only a 25-minute boat trip from the old port of Helsingborg to Helsingör in Denmark.

Skåne has Sweden's richest farms set in a landscape of rich colour. The magnificent coastline offers beaches, fishing villages, skerries for sea-fishing, and, on the **Bjäre Peninsula** to the northwest, rocks shaped like statues at **Hovs hallar.**

To the west of Skåne is the south's most fashionable resort, **Båstad,** best known for its international tennis events. **Torekov,** a former fishing village at the tip of the Bjäre peninsula, has also turned into a chic resort while retaining its picturesque atmosphere.

From here it's a short trip by boat to **Hallands Väderö,** an island nature reserve harbouring some interesting birdlife and flora. Many coastal stretches are a bird-watcher's paradise, and there are also several good bird lakes inland, such as **Ringsjön,** northeast of Lund.

Falsterbo in the far southwest is a typical example of the Swedish coast's fine beaches.

The south's long-established wealth is reflected in more than 250 castles and historic buildings. A good example, standing on an island in Lake Ringsjön, is **Bosjökloster.** Dating from about 1080, this former Benedictine convent boasts a fine 12th-century church, fine gardens, and parkland, as well as a thousand-year-old oak tree, a rose garden, and a small zoo.

In addition, many towns are fortified—Helsingborg's medieval keep, **Kärnan,** the only one of its kind in Sweden, is just one example. **Landskrona,** farther south, has a **Citadellet** that dates from 1549.

On the southwestern side of Skåne are two friendly summer resorts, **Falsterbo** and **Skanör,** while fine scenery awaits you on the east coast.

Ferry routes link **Trelleborg,** on the south coast, to the German ports of Travemunde, Rostock, and Sassnitz. Farther on, **Ystad** boasts rare old houses in a near-Tudor style, and is also the ferry departure point for the Danish isle of **Bornholm.** To the east, the tall rock of **Stenshuvudet** rises majestically from the Baltic above a landscape that contains more fruit farms and orchards than any other part of Sweden.

Another great fortification from the early wars is the 15th-century **Glimmingehus,** southwest of **Simrishamn,** which is regarded by some as Scandinavia's

Glimmingehus, perhaps Sweden's best preserved medieval fortress.

best preserved medieval fortress. Some of these old buildings are now hotels; others are used for folk dancing and cultural events.

Malmö and Lund

Malmö, south of Helsingborg on the west coast, is a rare mixture of old and new, with just under 250,000 citizens. Like most ports, the influence of immigrants from many parts of the world has given it a cosmopolitan, jaunty air—one in five Malmö residents has a foreign background. The renowned filmmaker Ingmar Bergman was once the director of the theatre here.

Stortorget (central square) is huge, and has a fine **Rådhus** (City Hall). Here, too, is one of the earliest houses in Malmö, **Jörgen Kocks hus,** which dates from the early 16th century. Just off the square to the east is the lovely, 14th-century **St. Petri's Kyrka,** replete with treasures from the 16th and 17th centuries. Danish king Kristian III built **Malmöhus** when Skåne was still part of Denmark; it now houses museums.

The Malmö **tourist office,** north of Stortorget and opposite the Central Station, runs guided tours; and public bus number 20 is equipped with information to help visitors pinpoint sights. For a restful break, try **Pildammsparken,** Sweden's largest landscaped park, with an amphitheatre used for summer performances.

The **Konserthuset** is the base of the Malmö Symphony Orchestra. In August, the big **Malmö Festival** attracts large crowds, as does the nearby **Jägersro,** Sweden's only combined trotting and race track, and the venue for the Swedish Derby, also in August.

Skåne's poppy fields add rich colour to "Sweden's Granary."

Fruits, flowers, vegetables, and more can be had at Möllevångstorget, Malmö's best street market.

Lund, 25 km (15 miles) or so northeast of Malmö, is a gracious university city with winding, cobbled streets, old buildings, and an atmosphere of age and learning. It is believed to have been founded by Danish King Sven Tveskägg ("Fork beard") in 990; in 1020 his son King Canute began to turn it into a political, cultural, commercial, and religious centre. By 1103 it had become the seat of the Archbishop of all Scandinavia and Finland. Lund's towering Romanesque **Cathedral,** which was consecrated in 1145, has a fine altarpiece dating from the 15th century. Its **Astronomical Clock** shows the movement of the heavenly bodies, the paths of the sun and moon, and, for good measure, the journey of the three wise men to Bethlehem.

Lund University, which was founded in 1666, is set in beautiful gardens. Its 30,000 students form an important part of Lund's modest population of 120,000, and are particularly noticeable on such special occasions as Walpurgis night (see page 88).

Lund has good museums; worth visiting are the **Lunds Konsthall** (Art Gallery), the **Historiska Museet,** and the **University Library,** as well as the **Kulturhistoriska Museet** (Museum of Cultural History).

Blekinge

The Swedish writer Selma Lagerlöf (see page 61) described Blekinge as the land of three steps—coast, inland, and forest—and today it is known as "Sweden's Garden." It has a string of small towns with long histories, and a lovely archipelago with countless islands. Inland, the forest once acted as a refuge for outlaws from the border wars; it is dotted with small, well-concealed villages. This miniature province is in fact something of a microcosm of Sweden, right down to its famous salmon river and good golf course.

Blekinge's largest town, 17th-century **Karlskrona,** has had a long association with the Swedish Navy. Its wide streets, old buildings, and fortresses have a flavour of the sea—not least because it is built on 30 islands—and it offers excellent facilities for boating, fishing, and swimming. **Marinmuseet** (the Maritime Museum) has a splendid collection of ships' figureheads, and the training ship **Jarramas** can be seen tied up at one quay.

On the E22 into Blekinge from Skåne in the west, small towns are found mostly on, or near, the coast. The exception is **Olofström,** 30 km (21 miles) north on the Skåne border. This town has a 19th-century spa, **Jämshög,** close by, and an interesting old water- and saw-mill on **Lake Halen,** which is also good for bathing.

There are a number of towns close to the coast of Blekinge. In medieval **Sölvesborg,** the ruins of **Sölvesborg Slott,** a castle from the 13th century, draws visitors, and **Mörrum** (on the **Mörrumsån,** a superb salmon river) attracts anglers from near and far. **Karlshamn** is notable for its **Emigrants' Monument,** a moving tribute to those who left their homes for a brave new world across the ocean (see page 21), while **Ronneby,** a 19th-century spa, is now Sweden's biggest conference and recreation centre.

Småland

Fly from Stockholm to the east coast city of Kalmar and you will see Småland below as a stretch of green forest studded with hundreds of small blue lakes and lighter patches comprising fields and villages. Driving along the roads through those forests, the pine and birch stands open out into moorland and small towns. Småland has always been an area of smallholdings, where "crofters" lived off an ungrateful soil; it has bred a tough, determined people.

The province has given birth to many of Sweden's notable figures, including the Father of Botany, Carl von Linné (Linneaus), tennis players Mats Wilander and Stefan Edberg, soprano Jenny Lind (the "Swedish Nightingale"), and writer Astrid Lindgren (see page 48).

From Småland also came the majority of the one million people (around one-quarter of Sweden's population at

Bicycles await their riders outside of Donkyrka, Kalmar's historic cathedral.

that time) who sailed to the New World, and even today Små-land celebrates Minnesota Day in August.

Kalmar is an ancient city, first noted on an 11th-century rune stone, while the formidable **Kalmar Slott** has long guarded the straits between the mainland and Öland. Built on 12th-century ruins, the castle dates from the time of Erik XIV (crowned in 1561). It was here that the Kalmar Union was signed in 1397 (see page 16). Kalmar was also one of the trading ports of the powerful German Hanseatic League (see page 14).

Kalmar Slott is now the last resting place of what remains of the royal ship *Kronan*. In May 1676, when Sweden was at war against a Danish-Dutch fleet, Admiral Lorentz Creutz

---

A Daring Raid

Until 1658 the border between the provinces of Blekinge and Småland was Sweden's uneasy frontier with Denmark. Marked by the small community of Kristianopel, once a Danish fortress, the area was fought over for centuries. Then, the icy winter of 1657–1658 gave Sweden's King Karl X Gustav his chance...

Arctic weather froze the sea between Sweden and Denmark and the Great Belt separating Denmark's first and second islands. Although already at war with Poland and Russia, Karl Gustav sent his troops on to the ice. Two squadrons of horses and riders fell through and drowned, but 5,000 foot soldiers and 1,500 cavalry reached Denmark's central island, Fyn.

Despite a thaw, they followed that journey with an even more hazardous crossing to Denmark's main island, Sjælland (Zealand), and reached the walls of Copenhagen. Denmark had no choice but to agree to the Treaty of Roskilde and cede its northern provinces on the mainland to Sweden. They have remained Swedish ever since.

was tucking into a substantial lunch when news was brought that the enemy was close by. The admiral turned his ship to engage the enemy, but turned too swiftly. The sails plunged sideways, water rushed in, and something fired the magazine. The blinding explosion blew out one side of the vessel and, of the crew of 842, only 42 souls survived.

A diving team found the *Kronan* in 1980, and its treasures have gradually been retrieved, including the ship's bell, cannon, and compass, and some 300-year-old brandy.

The northern archipelago referred to as the **Blue Coast,** where Småland shades into Östergötland, offers fishing villages, beaches, and hundreds of islands and harbours for all kinds of watersports. **Västervik,** 130 km (90 miles) north of Kalmar, an excellent starting-point for deep-sea fishing, has a popular **Ballad Festival** during the summer. Ferries to

---

Astrid Lindgren and Pippi Longstocking

Astrid Lindgren, author of *Pippi Långstrump,* was born in 1907 in Vimmerby in northeast Småland, which has now become almost a place of pilgrimage for both children and parents.

Astrid Lindgren did not plan to sell her writing. She first made up the stories for her young daughter, telling her of the adventures of Pippi Longstocking, a small girl who was full of charm but lonely. Once published, these enchanting tales quickly became favourites in more than 30 languages.

Astrid Lindgren has written some 50 books, but no character has become as popular as the original Pippi. Lindgren's success was such that, in 1976, the Swedish authorities assessed her taxes as 102 percent of her income. The result was a rare move by Lindgren into adult fiction, with a rapier-sharp satire on the bureaucracy of an "imaginary" dictatorship.

Gotland leave from here and from Oskarshamn, the main terminal farther south.

Heading inland on Highway 33 from Västervik will bring you to **Vimmerby,** birthplace in 1907 of the much-loved children's writer, Astrid Lindgren. Celebrating her works here is **Saga Town,** which consists of miniature buildings, all authentic copies of the places she wrote about. They offer an excellent introduction to her characters and stories.

The Kingdom of Glass

Away from the coast, hidden in the forests, is Småland's most famous industry. Ranging from the small glassworks at **Pukeberg** to such famous names as **Kosta** and **Orrefors,** 16 highly profitable glassworks lie near the 80-km (50-mile) stretch of Highway 25 between Nybro and Växjö.

As well as building Kalmar Slott, in 1556 King Gustav Vasa brought glass-blowers to Sweden, but another 200 years were to pass before glass came to Småland. The province had wood for the furnaces, and, when Karl XII rewarded two of his generals with the governorship of Småland, they set up the first glassworks. Taking the first syllables of their surnames (Anders KOSkull and Georg Bogislaus STAel von Holstein), *Kosta* was born. Today, most companies welcome visitors during the summer months to watch the skill in turning a glowing mass of molten glass into exquisite shapes; most have shops selling glass at bargain prices. Some will also arrange special Hyttsil Evenings (see

An ethereal exhibition of designer glass by Orrefors in Småland province.

page 100), which hark back to the days when herring was cooked in the heat from the furnaces. Another industry that owes its lifeblood to this area is furniture-making. Much of the furniture that is bought in the distinctive IKEA stores all over Europe and the United States comes from Småland.

In **Växjö,** 109 km (68 miles) northwest of Kalmar, there is a good **Glasmuseet** (Glass Museum). But its main claim to fame is the **Utvandrarnas hus** (House of the Emigrants), which holds the largest archive on emigration in Europe. One of its founders was Vilhelm Moberg, author of the best work on the great exodus, *The Emigration Trilogy,* which was later made into two films.

Northwest of Växjö, close to the border with Halland, **Värnamo** has an **Open Air Museum** with a collection of old buildings. Approximately 25 km (18 miles) farther on, near **Anderstorp,** is Småland's version of the Wild West, a ranch-style park called **High Chaparral** located out in the forests. The northernmost tip of this large province's most fertile area stretches to the southern end of Lake Vättern (see page 61).

The Islands

The two southeastern Baltic islands, **Öland** and **Gotland,** are very different in style and character both from the mainland and each other. Öland is long and narrow, connected to Kalmar on the mainland by one of Europe's longest **bridges,** with slender arches stretching for just over 6 km (almost 4 miles), while Gotland, 120 km long and 40 km at its widest (90 by 30 miles), is the Baltic's largest island. Gotland claims the longest hours of sunshine in Sweden—500 from 15 June to 15 August.

Öland

The remarkable bridge that stretches between the mainland and Öland transports you to a different scene altogether.

The great bridge to Öland from the mainland offers wonderful views of water and islands.

Öland is its own world, with the huge limestone plateau of **Alvaret,** a botanist's dream with wildflowers galore, including 40 species of orchid.

Borgholm, the first town over the bridge, and **Borgholm Slott** are worth lingering over. **Öland Zoo,** lying just below the bridge, has long been patronized by the Royal Family, who stay on Öland at **Solliden,** their summer home.

Above all, this is an outdoor island and birding country. Visit **Ottenby Observatory,** at the southern tip of the island next to **Långe Jan,** Sweden's tallest lighthouse. Ottenby is popular with bird watchers because of the migrants, such as honey buzzards, which can sweep past in huge numbers.

In prehistoric times, people lived in the safety offered by the island, although only their burial grounds remain now. Of great interest is the fortified village of **Eketorp,** which has been restored to show the life of a busy community between A.D. 300 and 1300. The ruined walls of **Gråborg Castle,** 8.5

The stunningly preserved architecture of Visby makes it the perfect setting for the annual Medieval Week.

metres (25 feet) high and in places almost as wide, hint at the size of this sixth-century fortress.

Gotland

The first modern outsiders to discover Gotland were writers and artists, such as Strindberg, Selma Lagerlöf, and Carl Larsson. Gotland is often called the *Island of Roses and Ruins*, thanks partly to its deep red roses, which are in bloom as late as November. Everything grows here; **Almedalen,** the former Hanseatic harbour in Visby, is now a lovely garden park with graceful plants in reed-lined pools. In summer the modern harbour is filled with masts while boat-owners lounge in outdoor cafés.

Visby was once an important trading centre in the Hanseatic period (see page 14), the German legacy of which shows in the town's architecture. In total, 3 km (2 miles) and 44 towers remain of the medieval walls. By sad contrast, the Gothic **St. Catherine's Church** is now a ruin beside the market square.

Within the old walls, much of the medieval city still stands —step-gabled houses with red pantile roofs, narrow streets, buildings like **Gamla Apotek** (chemist's shop), which now sells silverware, and the three towers of **Domkyrkan Sankta Maria** (the cathedral).

Gotland still possesses 90 medieval churches, a tribute to the wealth of the farmers in the years before Visby gained the trade monopoly. Every year in August, Medeltidsveckan (Medieval Week) turns back time; Gotlanders don medieval costumes to revel as merchants, monks, and high-born ladies.

Like Öland, Gotland offers outdoor attractions. The largest forest, Lojstaskogen, still has a wild herd of an unusual breed of ponies with two toes, called *Russ* since they are believed to have come from Russia (*Ryssland* in Swedish). There are also two good bird islands just south of Visby.

North of Visby, one of the island's best sights is found at **Lummelundagrottorna,** where the magnificent limestone caves are lined with huge stalactites.

Fårö, a small island off the north of Gotland, is a military zone, but it has been open to foreigners since 1992 (with the exception of its southernmost tip). From Rute in Gotland visitors must proceed straight through to Fårö Church, but can then wander freely around the old village. You will also be able to see the *Raukar* stone formations here.

GOTHENBURG AND THE WEST

The most exciting way to arrive in Gothenburg is by sea, standing on deck as the land creeps towards you. The ship heads through a maze of small islands and into the mouth of the Götaälv, past the ruins of Elfsborg Fortress, which once guarded this entrance. Ahead is the high curve of the Älvsborg Bridge; at night the scene glows with lights.

Sweden's largest passenger and cargo harbour is transited by some four million travellers each year. It is changing, too, as many of the shipyards that closed in recent years are now being redeveloped into commercial and residential properties.

The most obvious feature is the **Skanskaskrapan,** an office tower that looms over everything like a giant red-and-white funnel. On the 22nd floor, the **Utkiken** ("lookout") provides spectacular views of the city. On the other side of Lilla Bommen Hamn is the new **Göteborgsoperan** (Opera House), opened in 1994.

Houses are also starting to rise close to the water; the harbour is becoming a popular place to live. Along the south bank at **Packhuskajen,** vintage ships herald a **Sjöfartscenter** (Maritime Centre), where 15 historic vessels moored at the dock. It is part of the **Sjöfartsmuseet** (Maritime Museum), which is located farther down river in the **Masthugget** area. From the water the museum is picked out easily—in front stands a tender statue of a sailor's wife gazing out to sea on the 44-metre- (142-foot-) tall **Sjöfartstornet** tower.

Gustav Adolf's City

Gothenburg was founded in 1603 by Karl IX, next to what was then Sweden's only outlet to the western sea. The city huddled around Älvsborg Fortress, but this was captured by the Danes in 1612 during the Kalmar War. They ransomed it for one million Riksdalers, a huge sum that led to heavy taxes and took more than six years to pay, by which time the town had almost crumbled away.

The city was founded for a second time in 1619 by Karl IX's son, Gustav II Adolf; he is commemorated by a statue in

the square that bears his name, **Gustav Adolfs Torg.** Here he stands, pointing imperiously to the place south of the Götaälv where his new city was to rise.

Gustav saw Gothenburg as Sweden's western trading gateway; he enlisted Dutch builders, who designed a layout with moat and canals. Two canals remain to give Gothenburg its characteristic style, which is best appreciated by **Paddan Boat** (literally translated "Toad Boat") from Kungsportsplatsen.

Little of Gustav Adolf's city survived the fury of the periodic fires that razed the wooden buildings, and today Gothenburg is a fascinating jumble of dates and styles. The surviving buildings from those early days are all stone-built: the **Kronhuset;** part of the old wall, **Bastion Carolus Rex** at Kungsgatan; and the **Skansen Lejonet** and **Skansen Kronan** forts, the latter in the city's earliest suburb, Haga, just over 2 km (1½ miles) from the centre and now filled with military artefacts. The city remains compact, though, easy to see by foot, tram, or bus.

The Dutch-style Kronhus was built in 1643 as the city armoury. In 1660 it briefly became the House of Parliament, when Karl X Gustav died suddenly in the city and his four-year-old son came to the throne as King Karl XI. It is now the **Stadsmuseet** (or City Museum). In 1759, two rows of buildings were erected next door as workshops for the city artillery, and today they form the **Kronhusbodarna,** turn-of-the-centu-

The rivers and canals of Gothenberg provide a pleasant setting—both on and off the water.

ry workshops where you can buy craftware, breathe the aroma of spice, or nibble tasty old-fashioned cakes and buns.

On the west side of Gustav Adolfs Torg is the **Rådhuset** (City Hall), from 1672, and to the north **Börsen,** the old Stock Exchange. The first of the big canals, **Stora Hamnkanalen,** runs past the southern edge of the square, with fine mercantile buildings along its banks. On the north (Norra Hamngatan) is **Ostindiska Huset,** the Swedish East India Company's premises, now home to three museums, including the **Stadsmusset** (City Museum), documenting Gothenburg from the Middle Ages to the start of this century.

In contrast to all this history, northeast of Gustav Adolfs Torg is **Nordstan,** Sweden's largest shopping centre. An arcade now covers the old central street, leading to Central Station and the bus terminus.

Walking Down the Avenue

Avenyn (Kungsportsavenyn) is more like a French boulevard than a Swedish street. Lined with trees, shops, and cafés spilling on to the wide pavements, it is always full of people—musicians, vendors, or locals just out for a stroll and a chat. It starts at busy **Kungsportsplatsen,** where a statue of Karl IX stands before the main **Tourist Office.**

Crossing over **Rosenlundskanalen** (the Paddan Boat terminus), the second of Gothenburg's two canals, **Stora Teatern,** Scandinavia's only theatre specializing in light opera, ballet, and musicals (closed in high summer) is on the right. Behind it, **Kungsparken** lies along the canal. Opposite the theatre, Trädgårdsföreningen is a favourite park (see page 58). A little farther on, to the right off Avenyn, is the **Röhsska Museet** (Museum of Arts and Crafts), which has a notable exhibition of modern design. The **Lorensbergteatern,** next to the museum, stages dramatic performances.

At the south end of Avenyn is **Götaplatsen**—from where, atop its fountain, Carl Milles' statue of **Poseidon** gazes at the world. The square is flanked by Gothenburg's **Stadsteatern** (City Theatre; most events are in Swedish), **Konstmuseet** (Art Museum), **Konserthuset** (Concert Hall, and home to the city's Symphony Orchestra), and the **City Library.**

The **Konstmuseet** houses a wonderful collection of Scandinavian paintings, many from the Nordic Light period at the turn of the century, when young artists met at Skagen in north Denmark. This time is portrayed in *Hip, Hip, Hurrah*, PS Krøyer's depiction of the artists toasting one another. The museum also houses the Hasselblad Center, which features developments in the art of photography.

Parks and Excursions

Liseberg, Sweden's biggest and, many would have it, best amusement park, is beyond Götaplatsen; it first opened on the occasion of the Gothenburg Exhibition in 1923. It has continued to delight visitors ever since, with rides, restaurants, and theatres nestled amidst well-tended gardens.

Of all Gothenburg's garden parks, **Trädgårdsföreningen,** on the banks of Rosenlundskanalen, is the most popular. Founded in 1842, and the only one that's acquired a nickname (**Trägår'n**), it has beautiful statues, rose gardens, and the **Palmhuset,** a tropical glasshouse from 1878. Another humid place here is **Fjäril-shuset,** which is full of tropical butterflies.

Gothenburg's largest park, **Slottsskogen** (Castle Wood),

A vision of tranquility at Millesgården.

offers 137 hectares (340 acres) of hills, trees, and grass, reached from the centre via Linnégatan. Here you'll also find the **Naturhistoriska Museet** (Natural History Museum), the country's oldest **Deer Park,** and a children's zoo.

To the southeast, across Dag Hammarskjöldsleden, is Gothenburg's **Botaniska Trädgård** (Botanic Garden), with more than 4,000 species in its massive rock garden. On the way to Slottsskogen, stop at **Feske Kyrka,** a fine fish market housed in a church-like building on the north side of Rosenlundskanalen. It also has a good fish restaurant.

Gothenburg is Sweden's best-equipped city for sports, and locals are happiest either sailing in the archipelago or teeing off on one of the area's 24 golf courses. The **Scandinavium,** one of the largest arenas in Sweden, is also here, as is the **Åby Trotting Track.**

If you want to take to the water, boats leave from Packhuskajen for **cruises** around the archipelago, with jazz and other bands on board. Shellfish cruises are also offered on the *M.S. Poseidon*. From Stenpiren, cruises go to the **Vinga Lighthouse** in the islands, or to **Elfsborg Fortress** in the river.

The Coast

The coasts on either side of Gothenburg are ideal places for bathing and lazing. This whole region is popular with Swedes, who come to stay in their *stugor* (rustic summer retreats).

Bohuslän to the north is an ancient province, as attested by the Bronze Age rock carvings at **Tanum.** The best way to see these figures is on an evening visit organized by the **Vitlycke Hällristningsmuseum** (Rock Carvings Museum), when they can appear to stand out in an almost unearthly way.

North of Strömstad, in an area that has been Norwegian, Danish-Norwegian, and Swedish in turns, the Swedish-Norwegian frontier is marked by a fjord and a high bridge into

Apron, rubber gloves, baseball cap—an unlikely uniform for latter-day Swedish fishermen.

Norway. Just across the border on the Norwegian side, at Halden, is the remarkable ruin of Fredriksten Fortress, where King Karl XII met his death—an event that brought to an end Sweden's time as a great Baltic power (see page 19).

The small, thinly populated province of Dalsland, north of Bohuslän, has many lakes; it is a paradise for boat-lovers. The towns of **Bengtsfors** and **Dals-Ed,** which are really two villages joined by an isthmus with a lake on either side, enjoy some of the nation's most beautiful views. Weaving and winding its way through gentle landscape, the **Dalsland Canal** passes through locks and the awesome **Håverud Aqueduct** as it journeys on its way south to Lake Vänern.

Halland, to the south of Gothenburg, is a family favourite for its seaside towns, such as **Varberg**, **Kungsbacka, Laholm, Halmstad,** and **Falkenberg.** (Varberg and Halmstad have sea routes to Grenå in Denmark.) Inland is rich farming country. East of Kungsbacka, 26 km (18 miles) south of

Gothenburg, stands **Fjärås Bräcka**—a great ridge, formed by ancient glaciers, that looks over Lake Lygnern. Here, too, there are some large Bronze and Iron Age grave fields.

The Lakes

Sweden's great lakes lie to the northeast of Gothenburg. At 5,650 km² (or 2,180 square miles), **Lake Vänern** is the largest lake in Western Europe, while **Lake Vättern,** at 2,000 km² (750 square miles), is the second largest in Sweden. On the eastern side of Vänern is the Göta Kanal, which links with Lake Vättern *en route* to Stockholm.

In summer, these two huge lakes are dotted with boats and swimmers, and the shores with fishermen intent on hooking salmon. Vänern feels like a sea in the middle of Sweden, with Dalsland lying to the west and **Värmland** and **Västergötland** to the north and east. Värmland, along the Norwegian border, is wild and forested.

One of Sweden's most beautiful rivers, Klarälven, flowing south to join Vänern at Karlstad, is still used to float logs to the mills. Four-hundred-year-old **Karlstad** was once a trading post and a resting place on the pilgrim route, which followed the Klarälven north to the grave of St. Olav the Holy at Trondheim in Norway.

Two other lakeside towns are **Mariestad** to the east, with the towering spire of its 17th-century church, and, in the south, **Lidköping,** a porcelain town that holds a China Festival in August. Between the two is **Kinnekulle,** a beautiful 350-metre (1,150-foot) hill called the "flowering mountain."

North of Lidköping on the **Kållandsö Peninsula** is one of the finest castles Sweden has to offer, the restored 17th-century **Läckö Slott.** Great houses dot the areas close to the lakes; Värmland has two in particular. **Rottneros Manor,** on Lake Fryken, is considered by many the most beautiful in Sweden, while **Mårbacka,** on the other side of the lake, was the home of Swedish writer Selma Lagerlöf (1858–1940), the first woman to recieve a Nobel prize (1909), who brought fame to the area with books like *The Story of Gösta Berling*.

On the west shore of Lake Vättern, **Karlsborg** is dominated by a huge 19th-century fortress, including **Slutvärnet** —said to be Europe's longest building at 680 metres (2,230 feet). **Jönköping,** at the lake's southernmost point, was once a market town and is now the capital of north Småland (see page 47). The safety match was invented—and is still made—here; the old factory is now a museum. To the east is **Huskvarna,** where weapons were made 300 years ago. The smithies are now a craft centre.

The Göta Canal

Threading its way through the countryside from Gothenburg to Stockholm, the first section of the Göta Canal—from Gothenburg to Karlstad on Lake Vänern—opened in 1800.

Today, the Göta Canal is a classic pleasure route, especially popular with Swedes as a trip to mark a decade birthday (much celebrated in Sweden). Routed through the Great Lakes to Mälaren and the west coast, it takes in peaceful countryside and small towns where people turn out to watch the 19th-century canal boats negotiate the locks. *En route* here are sometimes visits to an old *Herrgård* (manor house) for lunch, and all along the way binoculars are out to watch the animals and birds on the banks or on one of the many small islands.

The canal boats run between Stockholm and Gothenburg (and back again) from mid-May to early September. The trip in either direction takes four to five days. Details are available from Rederi AB Göta Kanal, Hotellplatsen 2, Box 272, S-401-24 Göteborg; tel. (31)-80-63-15.

North from Jönköping on the lovely lakeside road is the idyllic little town of **Gränna**. This was the birthplace of aviator S.A. Andreé, who in 1897 tried to cross the North Pole in an air balloon. (His body was found on White Island in 1930). Each year Gränna celebrates the flight with balloon events; there are many related exhibits in the **Andrée Museet.** While here, try the local specialities: luscious pears, and *polkagrisar*, a red-and-white peppermint rock you can watch being made in one of the *polkagrisar* bakeries.

From Gränna it's just a short boat trip to the narrow isle of **Visingsö.** Here, horse-drawn carriages take visitors to 17th-century **Visingsborgs Slott,** which held prisoners during Karl XII's wars with Russia.

Farther north and, thanks to the Holy Birgitta, on a grander scale, is **Vadstena,** with its beautiful 14th-century church. Born in 1303 into the noble Folkunga family, Birgitta gave up temporal life at the age of 40 after bringing six children into the world. She moved to Rome, where she founded the St. Birgittine Order. After her death, her body was brought back to Vadstena. Ironically, more than a century later, Gustav Vasa, the architect of the Swedish Reformation (see page 17), built a great, imposing fortress castle nearby. Church and castle still stand here today.

The Göta Canal (see box opposite) is a classic route for pleasure-boating.

THE CENTRAL HEARTLANDS

Seven provinces link the south of Sweden to its vast northern stretches, taking in a swathe of countryside and wilderness from the Norwegian border to the Gulf of Bothnia. They are, going from south to north, the coastal provinces of Gästrikland, Hälsingland, Medelpad, and Ångermanland, and the inland provinces of Dalarna, Härjedalen, and Jämtland—the last two both great sweeps of forest, river, and rising mountains. Even though they are on the eastern side of the country, Medelpad and Ångermanland form the county known, oddly enough, as Västernorrland—or West Norrland.

Dalarna—the Folklore Province

Dalarna is the heart of all things Swedish, where the old traditions and costumes are as natural a part of "feast" days as they were 100 years ago. **Lake Siljan,** the largest of 6,000 lakes that legend says were gouged out of the landscape by a falling meteorite, is the symbol of these folklore traditions.

Indeed, nowhere is the feast of **Midsommar** (Midsummer) celebrated more enthusiastically than in the lakeside communities, where the wooden houses are painted a special dark red with white trim. Dancers kick their heels around the decorated Maypole into the summer night, boosting their energy with traditional dishes.

In June, local people in costume row long "church-boats" to **Rättvik Kyrka** at the southeastern end of the lake, recreating the times when this was the easiest way to journey in from outlying farms. The 13th-century church has some interesting paintings of Bible characters.

The towns around Siljan are all different. Perched above the lake and affording lovely views, **Tällberg** is one of the most popular holiday spots. **Nusnäs** is the main source of the

Dalahäst (Dalarna horse), a carved wooden horse painted bright red. During the summer you can watch the carving and painting in the small factory.

At **Mora**, **Zorngården** was the home of **Anders Zorn** (1860–1920), a painter whose lavish works were part of the National Romantic movement of the time. His studio is as he left it. Zorn was the friend of another Dalarna painter, Carl Larsson.

Bears at the **Grönklitt Bear Sanctuary** a bit farther north roam the natural forest of their large enclosures. Visitors walk along paths to special viewing platforms for a superb view of the bears and the surrounding countryside. The park is also a home to wolves.

Church-boats are still made on **Sollerön** island, and traces of the Vikings are found here in several early graves. Above the lake, the 514-metre (1,650-foot) **Gesundaberget** gives a fine view all round and is home to a southerly **Santaworld,** which offers a mixture of animals, toy workshops, and a resi-

The red houses of Dalarna flank Lake Siljan, where Midsommar is always passionately celebrated.

dent Santa. **Leksand**'s open-air theatre holds annual performances of **Himlaspelet,** a mystery play.

An Industrial Past

The area around Lake Siljan—and particularly around Falun, to the southeast—is a paradise for industrial archaeologists, thanks to the industries that sprang up in the wake of mining in the Bergslagen district, in the neighbouring province of Västmanland. Forestry, and textiles, too, have helped to shape this part of the country; many successors of the blast furnaces and giant waterwheels that powered the early mills still continue today, with hi-tech companies now complementing a spectacular industrial history dating from the early 16th century.

☞ The **Stora Kopparberget** (or great copper mine) at Falun is famous. Visitors to the mine don helmet and boots for a long underground tour that can only inspire admiration for early miners and the feats they achieved in harsh conditions.

Stora, the company that owns the mine, is the world's oldest, having been founded in 1288. It is sad that after 800 years of mining, production has recently come to an end. (Incidentally, the pigment used for the traditional dark red paint that coats most Swedish wooden buildings is based on copper from this region.)

Traditional Dalahäst (horses) are painted red like the local houses.

Close to Falun, **Sundborn** is the home of the painter Carl 🖝
Larsson (1853–1919). You can go on guided tours of his
house, as well as of **Sundborn Kyrka** and the parsonage,
both of which have paintings by the artist on show.

Coast and Countryside

Life in tiny (in Swedish terms) Gästrikland centres on its
main town, **Gävle.** Here you'll find a **Railway Museum,** including an 1874 coach of the veteran traveller, King Oscar II.

The main coast road, the E4, sets out across Sweden's im-
mense distances, passing Söderhamn and Hudiksvall (Hälsingland's two principal coastal towns), Sundsvall and
Härnösand on the Medelpad-Ångermanland border, and
Örnsköldsvik, 700 km (435 miles) north of Stockholm.

Up the coast are many small fishing villages, where Baltic
herring comes into its own—served with dill, or sometimes
smoked golden brown and called *böckling*. Not far north of
Gävle, herring from **Bonan** is particularly famous (and is
usually smelled before it's seen).

Söderhamn goes back to the 17th century, when it was
built as an army town (the armoury is now a museum). To the
west, **Bollnäs** has, since 1919, been the home of a favourite
Swedish sweet, a peppermint once boiled in a house kitchen.
Today you can still see it being made in this traditional way.

Dalarna may be known as the "folklore province," but it is
Hälsingland that plays host to the **Hälsingehambo,** Swe- 🖝
den's biggest folk-dancing competition. On an early June
morning in the Ljusnan valley north of Bollnäs, the fiddles
strike up *Hårgalåten* and 3,000 people begin dancing up the
valley towards **Järvsö.** They dance in several stages (with
bus rides in between) from 6:00 A.M. until 10:00 P.M.! Along
the route you'll find scores of dancers at the roadside taking
off their shoes to wriggle their toes in relief. The "Hambo"

ends happily with the best 100 couples dancing in a final competition at Stenegård, Järvsö's manor house.

Delsbo, farther north, rivals the Hambo with a fiddlers' rally in early July. Hundreds of fiddlers gather at the **Delsbostämman** folk festival.

The old, prosperous ironmasters of this area left their legacy in many places, including the **Galtström Bruk** (or ironworks) on the Ljungan, to the west of Sundsvall. Built in 1673 and closed in 1917, the whole site, from blast furnace and foundry to elegant manor house and workers' dwellings, is in excellent condition.

In the same valley, on the E14 from Sundsvall and Ånge, **Flataklocken** rises to 465 metres (1,500 feet). It is the true centre of Sweden, with a road to the top, an observation tower, and a panorama that stretches for miles. You can get a certificate to prove you have been in the village of Munkbyn near the foot of the hill.

The Legend of the Hälsingehambo

This feat of long-distance dancing has its origins in a weird and macabre legend from long ago. One day, so the story goes, a strange fiddler arrived to lead the villagers in their celebratory dance. No one knew him, but he played well and the dancers followed, little realizing that this was no human fiddler, but the Devil himself.

All day the dancing continued, as the fiddler urged on their tired bodies with alluring tunes. When daylight faded, still they followed him on the exhausting route up Hårgaberget, a local mountain. At the summit they danced on, spinning around in a circle that never broke. As daylight returned, however, all that remained was their skulls, whirling forever to form a ring that, it is said, you can still find shining white in the mountain rock.

of that way of life has gone from the islands, but from Övik it is still possible to see genuine fishing villages on Ulvön and Trysunda; they have a number of lovely old fishing chapels to visit.

Forest, Mountain, and River

Where the great rivers rise in the mountains of Härjedalen and Jämtland, close to the Norwegian border, you will come across some magnificent waterfalls. **Tännforsen,** west of Östersund, is the most famous in Sweden, with a drop of 30 metres (100 feet) in a massive white wall that later becomes Indalsälven.

Farther north, **Hällingsåfallet** has, over thousands of years, bitten and scraped into the surrounding rock face to form Europe's largest filled canyon. There is the thrill of white-water rafting on many of these rivers, as well as canoeing and some superb fishing.

The slopes of Härjedalen and Jämtland offer facilities for skiing, walking, and climbing, as well as mountain-biking and pony-trekking. The forests are carpeted with delicate flowers and abundant wild berries such as raspberries, blueberries, and *hjortron* (cloudberries)—all favourites in the great Swedish pastime of berry-picking.

This is the land where the elk is king. "Beware of Elks" is a familiar road sign, for the elk sometimes come down to the roadside at sunset or sunrise.

A variety of other animals might be seen, including otters and beavers—and, well hidden in the remoter areas, lynx and wolverines. Bird watchers may catch sight of ravens, eagles, and some unusual species of owl. **Sånfjället National Park,** which lies on the south side of Highway 84 in Härjedalen (northwest of Sveg), contains the largest population of wild bears in the country, running expeditions to see them.

*In Jämtland, snow means skiing at resorts such as Åre,
located just below Åreskutan's great heights.*

Härjedalen is the highest province in Sweden, with the
highest village, **Tännäs,** and the highest A-road (84), which
runs over the **Flatruet Plateau.** From here you can get a
good view of Sweden's most southerly glacier on **Helagsfjäl-
let,** just east of the Norwegian border. At 1,796 metres (6,000
feet), this is the highest peak south of the Arctic Circle.

The way into these wild, isolated spots is from the south on
Highway 45 or east–west from Hudiksvall on Highway 84,
following the course of the River Ljusnan. The two highways
intersect at **Sveg,** Härjedalen's main town. Sveg's open-air
museum, **Gammelgården,** has 20 old buildings. The **King's
Stone,** erected in 1909, marks the arrival of the railway in the
town, while the railway bridge over the quiet waters of the
Ljusnan is truly a masterpiece of engineering. A relaxing way
to travel into Härjedalen and Jämtland is by rail, with good
links from the south. For railway connoisseurs, the scenic *Inlandsbanan* line (see page 125) heads north from Östersund.

☞   **Lake Storsjön** is to this area what Lake Siljan is to Dalarna. Sweden's fifth-largest lake, it lies right in the centre of the two provinces, with the old island of **Frösön** linked by a bridge to the main town of **Östersund,** founded by Gustav III in 1786.

Frösön is named after Frö or Frej, the goddess of fertility, from the long-ago days when islanders worshipped the Norse Gods. At the Frösön end of the bridge you will find the country's northernmost rune stone, which is 1,000 years old.

Frösö Kyrka, built over a sacrificial grove of the ancient Æsur religion, is popular for weddings. Every summer Frösön is the venue for performances of the well-known Viking story *Arnljot,* turned into an opera (one of five) by the composer Wilhelm Peterson-Berger (1867–1942), who lived here. Frösön also boasts a **Zoo and Tropical House,** with more than 500 animals. A trip to the top of **Frösö Tornet,** some 468 metres (1,560 feet) high, will reward the climber with superb views.

The oldest coal-fired steamship still in use in Sweden, the *S.S. Thomée,* plies the lake, the depths of which are said to conceal a creature along the lines of Scotland's Loch Ness monster. Many sightings have been claimed, but its existence has not been confirmed so far. For the curious, there is a display of monster-catching gear in the **Länsmuseet.** The beast itself is described as "a snake between 6 and 12 metres (20 and 40 feet) long, with humps and a small head."

Close to Norway, the mountains rise to around 1,800 metres (6,000 feet). This is a fine area for trekking and skiing, the season for the latter sometimes lasting well into summer on the high peaks. Härjedalen was one of Sweden's earliest resort areas; it has the country's oldest mountain hotel at **Fjällnäs.** Also here are classic resorts, among which are **Tänndalen, Bruksvallarna,** and **Ramundberget.** These are reached via Highway 84 from Sveg.

Farther north, in Jämtland, **Åre** is one of the finest modern ski resorts in the country. The town lies on the slopes of the 1,240 metres (4,500 feet) **Åreskutan,** which towers above it. Skiers are taken by funicular railway from the centre of the town to a point halfway up the mountain, from where a cable car carries them the rest of the trip to the summit. On Åreskutan, you could literally be on top of the world.

Lappland's oldest church at Jukkasjärvi; inside here are brilliant altar paintings.

NORRLAND AND THE ARCTIC

Norrland (the old Swedish name for "The North") covers the provinces of Västerbotten and Norrbotten, reaching east to the Gulf of Bothnia and the huge tract that is Lappland bordering Norway to the west—in all, a third or so of Sweden, with endless summer light and long, dark winters.

This is a remote area, with one third lying beyond the Arctic Circle—a fact that only acquires real significance as you travel the long moorland miles between the small communities, journeys punctuated by the gleam of lake or river, the heavy scent of the forest, or sunlight catching the mountain peaks to the west.

The largest towns in the Norrland area lie along the coast at the mouths of Sweden's great rivers, since only by river could timber be brought down to the mills on the coast. When the roads came, it was natural that they should follow the same course.

Norrland is the heartland of the Sami, a people who have wandered this wild territory since time immemorial. They were originally called Lapps—hence Lappland—but more recently Sami has become their preferred name.

The Sami in Norrland are divided into Forest Sami and Mountain Sami. The first live in the forest all year round, but the Mountain Sami wander far and wide, following their reindeer between winter pastures in the east and summer grazing in the west. In the past, Sami culture was neglected—schoolchildren, for instance, were taught Swedish rather than Sami—but that has now changed. Sami organizations promote the language and culture, and there is an (advisory) Sami Parliament.

The Sami People

The Sami have hunted wild reindeer—one of the only animals that can survive on the Arctic's sparse vegetation—since before the 16th century, and today this way of life acts as an effective method of reindeer management. Of the 8,000 Sami in Sweden, about a quarter of them make a living from reindeer.

Although life is still dictated by the reindeer, the Sami have adopted modern ways to ease their task: nowadays they herd with the aid of radios, dogs, and motorcycles or snowscooters. They have kept the tradition of Sami communities, however, dividing themselves into Sami villages based on collective groups of reindeer owners who work together. The result may be that a community is not necessarily all in one place.

The Sami count, divide up their herds, and mark the calves over two or three weeks during the summer, colourful occasions with lots of flying lassoes and careering reindeer. Most Sami people welcome visitors to watch—bear in mind, however, that this is not a spectacle, but the Sami way of earning a living.

Their great annual gathering is at the Jokkmokk market, held in the month of February (see page 80).

Coast and River

Driving north on the E4 will bring you to the coastal town of **Umeå,** Norrland's largest, with a population of 93,000. Founded in the early 17th century in Gustav II Adolf's great expansion, it has become home to Norrland's only university and emerged as a significant cultural centre since the 1970s. Its suc-

Some 2,000 Sami still make their living from reindeer, a year-round way of life.

cessful Chamber Music Festival, held each June, is now linked with the Finnish Korsholm Festival just across the Gulf. It also hosts the International Jazz festival in October.

In one of the periodic wars between Sweden and Russia, at least 1,000 houses in Umeå were destroyed, and, in the war of 1808–1809, when Sweden lost Finland to Czar Alexander, the town suffered heavily when Russian soldiers attacked from across the ice (old bullet holes can still be seen at the idyllic harbour of **Ratan**).

Gammlia is one of the oldest open-air museums in Sweden, dating from 1920. It also has the area's main museum, with a fine Sami exhibit and notable buildings from the region. The island of Holmön is Sweden's largest and sunniest offshore nature reserve, free of cars and with bicycles for hire.

As you head north, you'll see reminders of the old industries—some now museums, others still working side by side with new, hi-tech enterprises. Church villages, from the days when a church served many far-flung communities, can also be seen. In **Lövånger Kyrkby,** between Umeå and Skellefteå, 100 well-restored church cottages now house visitors.

Skellefteå, though largely industrial, offers the miniature world of **Lilleputlandet.** A big summer festival is celebrated in **Bonnstan Kyrkby,** which has a 100-year-old steam tug, *S.S. Nordkust.*

From Skellefteå to **Piteå,** over the border in Norrbotten, the E4 clings to this beautiful coast, offering views of islands and headlands. **Öjebyn** has a church village dating from 1621, while Piteå, a little farther north, is largely devoted to paper and pulp mills. Its mild climate has earned it the nickname of the Norrland Riviera, and the warm Gulf waters certainly attract many visitors to sea resorts such as **Pite Havsbad,** with a beach, bathing, and a campsite.

As an alternative to the coast route, turn northwest on road 374 to Älvsbyn and then continue on up to Bredsel and **Storforsen,** claimed to be Europe's highest falls with a spectacular unbroken drop of 80 metres (250 feet). Returning to Älvsbyn, take road 356 to **Boden**—Sweden's largest garrison town, a fortress built after the 1808–1809 war. (Parts of Norrbotten near this border are military areas subject to entry restrictions; details are given on road signs.) From Boden, Highway 97 runs alongside Luleälven to Luleå.

The 300 islands forming the **Luleå Archipelago** are among the most beautiful in Sweden. **Luleå** itself is surrounded on all three sides by water. First founded by King Gustav II Adolf 10 km (6 miles) farther up the estuary, the first harbour was too small; almost 30 years later, Luleå moved to the site it occupies today. The old town, **Gammelstad,** is now a church village, with 30 old farms and 450 cottages clustered round a 15th-century granite church.

From Luleå, the E4 passes quite close to the northernmost waters of the Bothnian Gulf at **Kalix,** where the church has endured a turbulent history. Built in the 15th century, only the altar screen and font survived a fierce early fire. After rebuilding, it was ransacked in 1716 by Russians, who used it as stables in the 1808–1809 war. Victims of this war, both Swedes and Finns, are buried in the graveyard.

At **Sangis,** on the way to Haparanda, an archaeological dig in 1923 revealed a **Viking Grave.** The grave contained a warrior buried with his sword and shield, which are now in Norrbottens Museum in Luleå. The museum also houses a fine collection of Sami ethnography. To the north is the Sami town of **Överkalix.**

When the treaty that ended the 1808–1809 war left Sweden no access to Tornio at the mouth of the Torneälven, the Swedes promptly built **Haparanda** on the west bank—for nearly 200 years Sweden's easternmost town, and today the starting point for an almost unlimited number of outdoor pastimes in the wilderness to the north.

The Inland Way

There are two scenic routes for travel in Sweden's northern interior: by **Inlandsvägen** (road route, starting in Gothenburg) or **Inlandsbanan** (rail, from Mora; see page 125). Detours are easier by car, but most Swedes use the train rather like a bus, leaving it for outdoor pursuits and rejoining it later.

The **Vildmarksexpressen** (Wilderness Express) offers a special guided train tour from Östersund to Arvidsjaur, some 380 km (228 miles) north, with a choice of stops and pursuits. At Gällivare the *Inlandsbanan* merges into the great east coast route from Stockholm (a long 16 hours away, best by sleeper). The route then continues to Kiruna and the border, 200 km (130 miles) to the north.

Sundsvall, on the Gulf of Bothnia, is largely stone, risen from the ashes of the Great Fire of 1888, which destroyed half the town. It was rebuilt in style by timber barons.

Several northern towns on the Gulf of Bothnia suffered in Swedish-Russian conflicts. After **Härnösand** was raided in 1721, few of the early buildings were left apart from the wooden houses in **Östanbäcken.** The best view of town and harbour is from **Murberget** open-air museum, second only to Stockholm's magnificent Skansen (see page 33).

Just north of Härnösand is a memorial to the strikers shot by soldiers during the Hungry Thirties (see page 22). The statue, by sculptor Lenny Clarhäll, was erected in 1981 at Lunde, right at the southern end of the beautiful Sandöbro bridge.

Kramfors, 10 km (6 miles) farther north and on the same side of the river, is Sweden's accordionists' town, thanks to musician Kalle Grönstedt. It is also the home town of Frans Berwald (1796–1868), one of the first Swedish composers. Berwald was a violinist and infant prodigy who played in Stockholm's Court Chapel when still a child.

Härnosand is the beginning of a little-known part of this coast that is too good to miss, the beautiful **Höga Kusten** (High Coast), stretching 80 km (48 miles) north to Örnsköldsvik, with the **Nordingrå peninsula** as its centre.

The High Coast may have remained a secret because it is hard to see from the E4. The simplest detour is to turn right off the road at Gallsäter into a world of high cliffs, inlets, bays, and islands. Here are tiny villages, wonderful places to swim, and little restaurants where you can get a taste of *husmanskost* (home cooking).

At the northern end of the High Coast, **Varvsberget** rises out of the town of Örnsköldsvik (also known as Övik). The mountain affords a good view over the Gulf of Bothnia and nearby islands, home to the fishermen-farmers of old. Most

Starting from Östersund by car (Highway 45), the route to Dorotea lies through Jämtland (see page 70) and endless tracts of dense forest. Both road and rail run across dozens of small islands linked by bridges, and past lakes where you may see beaver and their handiwork.

Most small towns between **Dorotea** and **Arvidsjaur,** 250 km (150 miles) north, have a church, a local museum, and possibly a craft shop, giving a taste of the past. Dorotea's church has sculptures by the artists Carl Milles (see pages 34) and Björn Martinis.

In 1794, the principal town, **Vilhelmina,** was a church village with 241 people and 38 buildings, most of which have now been converted for summer visitors. The **Västerbottens Slöjd and Same Ätnam** (Västerbotten and Sami Crafts) is open for visits and sales. Vilhelmina is a place for folk dancing and singing, most notably during July's festive days, which include an old-fashioned wedding. If you travel by *Vildmarksexpressen*, you may well find your arrival greeted by folk musicians, and in minutes you could even be dancing on the platform.

Several villages lie at the junctions with east–west roads; at **Storuman** the road crosses the Blue Way (E12) from Umeå, so-called because of its many lakes. The heady panorama of lake, forest, and peaks visible from Storuman's **Utkiken** ("the lookout") will justify the name.

Heading north again for Arvidsjaur, those with a car can divert west at Slagnäs (beyond Sorsele) on to a minor road that skirts the lovely waters of Storavan and Uddjaur, to the Sami town of **Arjeplog.**

Almost surrounded by water, Arjeplog lies at the junction of this small road with the Silver Road from Arvidsjaur. Apart from its splendid setting, its highlight is the **Silvermuseet,** a paean to the silver mines nearby. It is best known

Have stick, will travel—Sweden's vast rural expanses are virtually a walker's paradise.

for a huge collection of Sami silver and illustrations of Sami life. The church, which also displays beautiful silver, is one of Norrland's oldest, founded in 1641 by Queen Kristina.

Arvidsjaur still has the feel of a frontier town—not just because it is a training-ground for army conscripts, but because it lies at the junction of five roads, and, 100 years ago, became a main trading post. This pretty town of 8,000 souls has a wide main street and lakes close to the centre. **Lappstaden** is the oldest preserved church village in the country, with 80 Sami *kåtor* (houses)—a monument to the Forest Sami who gathered here for markets and church festivals for hundreds of years. The Sami people celebrate a festival here, Storstämningshelgen, in late August.

Arvidsjaur is very much an outdoor place. **Piteälven** to the north is good for white-water rafting with the magnificent **Trollforsarna** (rapids); **Trollholmen,** an island that divides the river, is popular for walks, berry-picking, and picnics. The intrepid can take a course in hang-gliding; others may prefer to hire one of the old platelayer's trolleys, complete with camping equipment, and set off along the disused railway to Jörn, 70 km (50 miles) to the southeast. **Vit-tjåksfjällen** and **Prästberget** offer good skiing.

North of the Arctic Circle

Just before road and railway reach **Jokkmokk** (160 km/110 miles across marshland and forest to the north), you arrive at the Arctic Circle. Jokkmokk is in Sami territory; their great annual event, the **Jokkmokk Market,** first held here in 1605, takes place every year in the traditional spot at the beginning of February.

For three days people don bright traditional dress to meet and exchange news and have a good time. Visitors flock in to savour the Sami atmosphere and buy typical Sami handi-work, but you have to book a year ahead to be sure of a bed.

The town's **Ájtte** (museum) covers the culture and myths of the Sami, as well as the hard world of the 18th- and 19th-century Swedish settlers. *Ájtte* is the Sami word for a store-house, and this is indeed a fine store of artefacts, historical tableaux, and exhibitions, with a fascinating story to tell.

Southwest of Jokkmokk on Highway 97, **Vuollerim,** built around the excavation of a 6,000-year-old hunter settlement, displays well-preserved Stone Age tools and utensils. If you have an adventurous palate, Vuollerim serves the traditional dish of beaver.

Jokkmokk Kommun (district), the second largest in Sweden (roughly the size of Wales or Massachusetts), con-tains several vast national parks (of which **Muddus** is the closest to Jokkmokk town). It also boasts the country's wildest road, **Sjöfallsleden,** which branches northwest just after Porjus and passes through awe-inspiring scenery.

The road road ends 170 km (120 miles) farther at **Ritsem-jåkka,** high in the mountains, from where it is only another 18 km (11 miles) on foot to the Norwegian Sea (Atlantic).

From **Saltuluokta,** half-way along the route, a boat also follows Sjöfallsleden. All around is the magnificent wilderness of the **Sarek, Padjelanta,** and the **Stora Sjöfallet National Parks** (see pages 94–95).

Rail travellers to Gällivare will arrive at its very attractive 19th-century station. In nearby Malmberget, the **Gropen** is a huge pit that yields iron ore—like a scene from Dante's *Inferno.* It is the source of Gällivare's prosperity. Tour buses circle deep into the mine; the **Gruvmuseet** (mining museum) illustrates 250 years of local mining history. Settlers lived in **Kåkstaden,** which has now been restored.

The 825-metre (2,700-foot) summit of Gällivare's **Dundret** gives a view of just under 10 percent of the whole of Sweden. High up on one side of the mountain, a big holiday centre offers self-catering accommodation, camping facilities, restaurants, and swimming pools.

From Gällivare to Kiruna, rail and road part company, the latter merging into the E10 to Kiruna via **Svappavaara.** Here, Highway 45 comes into view again and heads northeast to **Karesuando**, which boasts Sweden's most northerly church, on the Finnish border.

Road and rail meet again at **Kiruna.** Until 1984, the road stopped here; the only way to Riksgränsen on the border with Norway was by rail. The road heads north along **Lake Torneträsk,** passing through some of the remotest and most beautiful scenery anywhere in the world. You can experience round-the-clock sunlight here from mid-June to early July.

Kiruna is a mining town of 27,000 people with a lake at its centre, set between two mountains packed with ore—Kirunavaara and Luossavaara. The first mining was by opencast methods, but most mining today is at depth; an underground tour (by bus) is dramatic; the machines resemble great prehistoric monsters.

The "father" of Kiruna must be Hjalmar Lundbohm, who helped plan the town's construction after his appointment as director of the newly-formed mining company in 1889. You can discover more about this progressive figure by visiting his home, **Hjalmar Lundbohmsgården.**

About 21 km (15 miles) east of Kiruna, **Jukkasjärvi,** on the Torneälven, is another world, with white-water rafting in the summer and impressive winter sports. In Sami, *Jukkasjärvi* means meeting place, which is just what it was for travellers of old on arduous treks through the great wilderness. Here is Lappland's oldest surviving wooden church, built in 1609, with a famous, brilliantly coloured altarpiece by Bror Hjort from Uppsala, an artist renowned throughout Sweden for his church paintings.

In winter, strangest of all is the **Arctic Igloo,** first built by local people in 1991. Each year since, as the **Arctic Hallen,** it has become a meeting place and gallery, with the Ice-Blue Bar —so-called because of the light it casts on the ice. Now, part of the igloo is used as a winter hotel for those who are unable to resist "something different"—although local innkeeper, Nils Yngve Bergqvist, whose idea this was, also has comfortable, warm, rooms in Jukkasjärvi's Wärdshus (inn).

At nearly 2,117 metres (7,000 feet), **Kebnekaise,** west of Kiruna, is Sweden's highest mountain; it makes a challenge even for experienced walkers. It can form the climax of a hike along **Kungsleden,** a fine route that runs 86

The still waters of Lappland's lakes make for fine fishing.

km (60 miles) from Abisko farther north, with overnight stops in mountain huts. This far to the north, from late May to late July, the sun never sets.

Whether by road or rail, the route to **Abisko Turiststation** (Abisko Mountain Station) is beautiful, offering views over the lovely waters of Torneträsk, and cutting through wilderness country with mountain peaks rising on both sides. The most noticeable heights are the twin summits that flank the deep semi-circle of **Lapporten,** the gateway to this last frontier.

Abisko has all the facilities for this outdoor life—full or self-catering accommodation, a shop, sports equipment, etc. As well as offering walking, mountain-biking, and skiing, the town is also the base for local guides who lead "specialist weeks" in topics such as botany, ornithology, and railway history. Next door is the **Naturrum,** a National Park station with an informative exhibition on the **Abisko** and **Vadvetjåkka National Parks** (see page 95).

Björkliden, some 7 km (5 miles) to the north, has the highest-altitude mountain station in Sweden. At 1,228 metres (4,000 feet), **Låktatjåkko** can attract skiers to its great 15 km (10 miles) of snow trails even in high summer; at this time of year you can also see beautiful, often rare, plants, some of them unique to Björkliden. In addition, the area has one of the country's best cave systems to explore. Nearby **Tornehamn** is a busy workers' settlement of the railway-building period. Its graveyard is the last resting place of those tough pioneers.

The last station in Sweden before you reach the Norwegian border is **Riksgränsen.** It is only 45 minutes by car or rail from the sea at Narvik; you can ski here at midnight in midsummer. The settlement is home to Sven Hörnell, one of Sweden's best nature photographers, whose inspiration is most obviously all around you.

WHAT TO DO

SHOPPING

High-class department stores in Stockholm, such as NK, Åh-léns, and Domus, now have branches in many towns. For a bargain, look out for the words *Rea* (meaning sale) and *Ex-trapris* (which does not mean *extra* but a special low price). In recent years, IKEA's stores, full of well-designed furniture and other household fittings, have become a Mecca for visitors, particularly those travelling by car. IKEA is usually located on the outskirts of cities.

Where to Shop

Each of the three main cities has its browsing area: Gamla Stan in Stockholm, the busy Avenyn in Gothenburg, and, in Malmö, a long, traffic-free zone that stretches along Söder-

Locally made clothing and handicrafts are abundant at Svenska Hemslöjden.

gatan from Stortorget. In addition, Gothenburg can boast the largest shopping centre in the country—the Nordstan.

Stockholm's **markets** are the colourful Östermalmstorg and Hötorget, where locals buy food. The southern district of Södermalm also has a market hall at Medborgarplatsen. In Gothenburg, Feske Kyrka was built as a church but is now a fish market, while *Saluhallen* (market hall) offers shops of all kinds. Malmö's *Saluhall* is a venerable old building at Lilla Torg, with restaurants, delicatessens, and cafés, and many of Malmö's squares have market stalls. The weekend **fleamarket** in Stockholm is held in **Skärholmen Center** (a 20-minute ride away by Tunnelbana), which claims to be the largest in Scandinavia.

What to Buy

Overall, your best bets are any of the following, reflecting Sweden's excellent design tradition. Also worth noting is Scandinavian chocolate, among the best anywhere.

Clothes: Clothes for both men and women are beautifully designed, but often expensive. Hennes & Mauritz is one exception on cost, specializing in fashionable clothing at reasonable prices.

Crafts: Svenska Hemslöjden is the place to go for good quality, locally made clothing and handcrafts, normally at reasonable prices. Gold and silver are usually good, and if you spot the signs *guldsmed* or *silversmed,* you might also find original designs.

Glass: Always a popular buy with visitors. The province of Småland is Sweden's "Kingdom of Glass" (see page 46) and home to famous names such as Kosta-Boda and Orrefors, as well as many smaller companies. In most of the glassworks you can pick up "imperfect" items for less than half the original price.

Porcelain: This comes to the big stores direct from the Gustavsberg factory situated outside Stockholm, and Rörstrand in Lidköping. Porcelain is by no means cheap, but the factories offer many good buys.

Textiles: Like porcelain, these can be expensive, but cheaper items can sometimes be found in factories. A good place from Gothenburg is Borås in *Tygriket* (Weaver's Country).

Tax-Free Shopping

MOMS, Sweden's version of VAT, is levied on most goods. It currently stands at around 25 percent, but more than 15,000 Swedish shops are part of a Tax-Free Shopping Scheme, aimed at non-Nordic countries' residents. This enables you to reclaim most of the tax paid on goods. Participating shops carry a Tax Free sign, and with each purchase you receive a cheque for the amount of VAT, less a small handling charge. You then claim your refund at Tax Free desks at air- or seaports (or sometimes on board ship) and at border crossings or service points in Denmark, Finland, and Norway.

ENTERTAINMENT

For a country of just 8.6 million people, Sweden boasts a very large amount of music, opera, ballet, and theatre in the larger cities as well as outlying areas. Theatre and concert tickets can often be bought at the kiosk at Norrmalmstorg in Stockholm.

Music, Opera, and Ballet

Classical music, opera, and ballet in Sweden compare with the best in the world. The **Konserthuset** is the venue for performances by the Stockholm Philharmonic Orchestra (the season runs from September to May or June), while *Sveriges Radio* (Swedish Radio) uses the **Berwaldhallen** as a base for its musical programme—the Radio Symphony Orchestra performs there regularly. Gothenburg's Konserthuset is home to the Gothenburg Symphony Orchestra. Malmö also has its Konserthuset where the Malmö Symphony Orchestra gives 50 concerts a year.

Stockholm's famous **Royal Opera House** (Operan) stages opera and ballet (late August to June); Gothenburg's **Stora Teatern** features light opera, musicals, and ballet, as does **Malmö Stadsteater,** which also offers theatre performances.

Unfortunately for summer visitors, regular theatre and concert performances stop during the Swedish holiday months, from late June to late July, though music is often offered in lovely alternative settings: the **Royal Palace** and **Drottningholms Slottsteater** in Stockholm, and **Liseberg** in Gothenburg—not forgetting **Malmöhus** in Malmö.

Outside the cities, Dalarna and other rural areas offer folk dancing. Scandinavians adore jazz and there are concerts and festivals all year round.

Gustav III built Damaten, Stockholm's main theatre, for the first play performed in Swedish.

Theatre and Cinema

For most visitors, language will prove a major problem at the theatre, as plays are more often than not performed in Swedish. However, Stockholm has an English Theatre Company, and the **Marionette Theatre** (Puppet Theatre) is another possible alternative. Almost all foreign films are shown in their original language with Swedish subtitles.

Nightlife

Swedes used to go home early. Today—in the cities at least—that's all changed, and nightclubs (some attached to the bigger hotels), dance restaurants, and discos may stay open to 3:00 A.M., particularly on Friday and Saturday. The rural areas, however, offer little late-night entertainment except in hotels.

With the very high price of drinks, a night out is always expensive; piano bars, jazz and rock clubs, or discos are often the best bet. Younger people should note that many nightclubs have surprisingly high minimum age limits.

Publications such as *Stockholm This Week* and *Malmö This Month* (free from tourist offices and some hotels and kiosks) list what's going on.

FESTIVALS

Swedes celebrate their festivals with zest. Though fewer attend church on Sundays than in days gone by, there is still a bedrock of traditional values.

Walpurgis Night and May Day (*Valborgsmässoafton och Första Maj*): Bonfires blaze for Walpurgis Night on 30 April, giving a feeling of the old Viking paganism in which the festival has its roots. It is a celebration of spring and the end of the long, dark winter. In the old capital city of Uppsala, students "sing in the spring" with traditional songs

Calendar of Events

Ask at local tourist offices for information on other events.

February. *Norrland:* Jokkmokk Sami Market, held since 1605.

April. *Gothenburg:* International Horse Show.

30 April/1 May. *Everywhere:* Walpurgis Night celebrations followed by May Day/Labour Day festivities.

June. *Everywhere:* Midsommar (Midsummer). Maypole dancing.
Everywhere: National Day on 6 June, marked with parades.
Stockholm: Archipelago Boat Day; steam boats to Vaxholm Island. Stockholm Marathon.
Motala: Vättern Round. World's largest cycle race.
Dalarna: "Church-boats" race on Lake Siljan.
Umeå: Umeå Chamber Music Festival.
Arjeplog: Lappland Music Festival.

July. *Stockholm:* Jazz and Blues Festival.
Marstrand: International Olympic class Boat Race.
Gothenburg: Gothia Cup. Football tournament (23,000 players).
Båstad: Swedish Open and Donald Duck Youth Tennis Tourneys.
Falsterbo: Falsterbo Horse Show.
Hälsingland: Hälsingehambo; long-distance dance competition.
Bjuråker: Folk Music Festival.

August. *Everywhere:* Crayfish and Sour Herring season begins.
Stockholm: Water Festival
Västergötland: Lidköping China (Porcelain) Festival.
Vaxjö: Minnesota Day, remembering Småland emigrants.
Malmö: Swedish Derby.
Visby: Medieval Week with costumed events.
Småland: Hultsfred Rock Festival, the biggest in Sweden.
Norrland: Jukkasjärvi Market from the 17th century.

September. *Norrland:* Umeå Jazz Festival (and October).

October. *Stockholm:* Lidingö; world's largest cross-country race.

December. *Stockholm:* Nobel Prize Day on 10 December.
Everywhere: St. Lucia Festival, 13 December.

Midsommar, held each year in June, is Sweden's biggest summer celebration.

and speeches. In the evening the town is alight with torch-lit parades and street parties. Rural areas are far more likely to celebrate May Day, with outdoor picnics, games, and competitions.

National Day (*Svenska Nationaldagen*): Swedes did come late to the idea of a special National Day, but 6 June was chosen because the great Gustav Vasa, who founded the Vasa dynasty, became king on 6 June 1523 (see page 16). Nowadays, there are parades throughout the country and a ceremony when the King and Royal Family (Queen Silvia in Swedish national costume) present flags to organizations and individuals.

Midsommar: This is by far the biggest summer celebration in Sweden; it was traditionally held on the solstice, but is now celebrated on the weekend nearest the 24th of June. Everywhere is decorated with flowers and greenery, and almost every community has its Maypole; the dancing goes on long into the night. On this day, pick seven different flowers from as many places, and place them under your pillow. You will dream, so they say, of your future wife or husband. Skansen in Stockholm and Liseberg in Gothenburg are excellent places to join in. Sweden's national maypole is raised in Leksand in Dalarna.

Lucia: The feast of St. Lucia of Syracuse on 13 December is Sweden's great winter feast, when communities around the country choose their own Lucia, all dressed in white with a crown of candles in her hair. She is followed by a train of white-clad girls and boys, and brings in a tray of coffee, saffron rolls, ginger biscuits, and *glögg* (mulled wine).

Sweden's national Lucia is crowned at Skansen, and there are special Lucia concerts all over the country. The festival, like so many in Sweden, has much to do with light; the glitter and candles symbolize a belief that, however dark December is, the light will return.

Music festivals: Sweden specializes in summer music festivals, with some 17 major events and many minor gatherings held in all parts of the country. This is a wonderful way to hear music, particularly in the north, in the long, light nights under summer skies. Many concerts are held in typically Swedish venues: castles, churches, and other historic buildings. Often, the music moves out of doors, and in the smaller communities everyone is involved.

Further details are available from Swedish Music Festivals, Rödhakevägen 3, S-906-51 Umeå.

The start of the Crayfish and "Sour Herring" season (*Kräft och Surströmmingspremiären*) in August is also worth noting (see page 98).

SPORTS

Swedes are true outdoor people, and you should find excellent facilities provided by the community in all places (less often by a private club or hotel).

Equestrian events: Riding is popular and most towns have stables and schools. There are many special treks for more experienced riders, ranging from day or weekend rides around Stockholm and Södermanland to mountain treks in Jämtland and Lappland, sometimes with hunting and fishing included. Ask for the leaflet *Equestrian Activi-*

ties, available from the Swedish Tourist Board in your own country (see page 123).

There are four major tracks for horse-racing and trotting in Sweden: in Täby and Solvalla (Bromma) in Stockholm, Åby in Gothenburg, and Jägersro in Malmö. The popular Swedish Oaks and Derby are both held at Jägersro, in July and August, respectively; and Gothenburg's International Horse Show is held at the Scandinavium in Gothenburg in April.

Fishing: Vast stretches of water make for fine fishing in lake, river, or sea. Superb salmon can be caught in lakes Vänern and Vättern, and even in central Stockholm, because the water is so pure. Freshwater fishing usually requires a permit, but sea fishing is free.

Further information may be obtained from Sveriges Sportfiske och Fiskevårdsförbund, Box 2, S-163-21 Spånga, Sweden; tel. (08) 795-33-50. In addition, the Swedish Travel and Tourism Council publishes *Fishing in Sweden.*

Golf is creeping up on tennis as one of the most popular sports in Sweden, with well over 300 courses. Most are private clubs, charging green fees, and some have special rules for visitors (for example, requiring an official handicap). In the north during summertime you can enjoy the rare experience of playing golf under the midnight sun. Further information is available from the Swedish Golf Federation, Post Box 84, S-182-11 Danderyd, Sweden; tel. (08) 622-15-00. Also, the Swedish Travel and Tourism Council publishes *Golf in Sweden.*

Skiing: In Sweden everyone skis as soon they can walk, and cross-country and downhill runs abound. One of the best resorts is Åre in Jämtland (see page 73), and in many areas you can ski all year round. Ski-touring is also popular.

Spectator Sports: Indoor and outdoor spectator sports, both at international and local level, include everything from tennis and golf to football, riding, and boat racing. Handball is popular, and some of the biggest tournaments are held in Stockholm. In June the capital plays host to one of Europe's biggest marathons. Dundret mountain at Gällivare in Lappland is the scene of a hang-gliding festival in early July.

Tennis: In the lingering wake of Borg, Wilander, and Edberg, there are many indoor and outdoor courts for public use throughout Sweden. Hotels may have tennis courts, but they are not a standard feature. Båstad, on Skåne's southwest coast, is the venue for the Swedish Open and the Donald Duck Club Junior Tournament (both held in July). Stockholm's Globe Arena hosts the Stockholm Open in October.

Walking: Walking takes pride of place alongside skiing as the Swede's preferred outdoor activity. Most popular are long-distance upland paths, such as Kungsleden in Lappland (see page 82), which attract hundreds every weekend, yet never become crowded. There are also forest tracks and space where *allemansrätt,* the law that allows wandering at will, can be enjoyed. You'll find mountain huts on most routes, and elsewhere wilderness camping is the attraction, especially in the National Parks (see pages 94–95).

Test your skills against the experts: join in the tennis fervour at the tournaments in Båstad.

Watersports: There are limitless possibilities, from swimming and canoeing to sailing and fishing. In summer, lakes Vänern and Vättern are dotted with boats, swimmers, and anglers. Every town has its indoor and/or outdoor swimming pool, plus a growing number of special adventure pools.

Windsurfing and waterskiing are increasingly popular, as is white-water rafting, particularly in the north. All over Sweden you can hire motor and sailing boats.

NATIONAL PARKS

Sweden's first four National Parks, all in Lappland, were opened in 1909. Largely wild mountain terrain with lakes and rivers, they cover huge stretches of land. The largest, **Padjelanta,** covers 198,400 hectares (some 490,250 acres) —a greater area than Lake Vänern.

The main objective of National Parks is to preserve Sweden's varied wild landscapes, and there are now 22 parks spread throughout the country, from Lappland to Skåne. They also offer one the chance to enjoy the tranquility of water, landscape, and wildlife.

One or two parks are total wilderness, where the Swedes

indulge their passion for getting back to nature, and where you can wander for days without seeing another soul. Others have footpaths, walking trails, accommodation, and even cable cars. **Sånjfället** in Härjedallen

In summer Swedes are happiest when they are either in or on the water.

has a bear population, and on the island of **Blå Jungfrun,** in the Kalmar Sound in Småland, legend tells that witches appear on the night of Maundy Thursday. Further information is available from the Swedish Environmental Protection Agency, S-171-85 Solna, Sweden; tel. (08) 698-000, and Svenska Turistföreningen, Box 25, Kungsgatan 2, S-10120 Stockholm; tel. (08) 463-21-00, fax (08) 678-19-58.

Svenska runs the country's youth hostels, mountain stations, and huts, which vary from basic shelters to large mountain stations with hotel-standard comforts. STF also owns 460 guest harbours (moorings).

CHILDREN

No child will go short of a Swedish **beach,** even in the heart of Stockholm, where the waters—salt or fresh—are pristine. The long west coast running north and south of Gothenburg provides endless swimming, as do the south coasts closer to Denmark. The sheltered waters of the Gulf of Bothnia are referred to as the Swedish Riviera.

Several country hotels and camping sites also have their own pools, plus sports and various **play areas.** In addition, there are numerous public play areas called *Parklek,* which provide bikes and tricycles, buckets and spades, and other toys, as well as attendants and tea and coffee.

The two great **amusement parks** in Sweden are Gröna Lund in Stockholm and Liseberg in Gothenburg. In the capital there is also the **open-air museum,** Skansen, with its fascinating old workshops.

Fjärilshus (Butterfly House), at Haga Park in Stockholm, has hundreds of tropical butterflies flying free. The **Marionettmuseet** offers glove puppets, marionettes, and masks. For a journey into space, try **Cosmonova** (only 15 minutes away by Tunnelbana to the *Universitetet* station).

The Technical Museum has a special **Teknorama** section for children.

Some **castles** also now have their own children's sections. **Läckö,** north of Lidköping on Lake Vänern, has a children's museum, and **Tidö Slott,** north of Mälaren, has a huge collection of dolls and toys. Around 130 km (80 miles) south of Stockholm, in Södermanland, is **Kolmården Wild Animal Park,** with a pets' corner and more than 100 animal species.

Malmö's and Gothenburg's **Little Trains** are a good way to get around, and old **trams** in Gothenburg are also great fun. **Almviks Djurfritidsgård** (or Almvik Children's Farm) is a genuine Skåne farm that was brought into the middle of a Malmö housing estate. Nearby is **Ak-va-Kul,** the largest water park in Scandinavia. Over on the east coast, **Saga Town** in Vimmerby is a celebration of the works of children's writer Astrid Lindgren.

In the north, there are three different types of **zoos** at Östersund, Junsele, and Lycksele, and unusual museums, such as the **Teknikens Hus** (Technical House) in Luleå, which keeps children occupied with hands-on exhibitions. If you're skiing, winter resorts such as Åre (see page 73) have good facilities for children.

Note for parents: Travel on Stockholm's buses is free for one parent if carrying one or more children in a pram or pushchair. Get on and off the buses using the middle doors, which are wide enough for double pushchairs.

Stockholm's Tjemilen race, when women dress up and run a "Swedish mile" (10 km/6 miles).

EATING OUT

I t has become easier to sample traditional Swedish dishes in restaurants because, in a sense, eating out has come full circle. Originally, most restaurants offered Swedish cuisine, but during the 1980s the restaurant scene went through something of a sea change when, in the cities certainly, it was easier to find French, Chinese, or Italian than local dishes. Now, some Swedish restaurants have regained the confidence to serve their native cuisine.

Where to Eat

Stockholm has more than 700 restaurants covering food from some 30 countries. In Skåne the motto is: "Plenty of food, good food, and food at the right time," so it is no surprise that Malmö claims to have more restaurants per head than anywhere else in Sweden.

Most top-class restaurants, which may be part of a hotel or independently owned, count the expense-account diner as their primary clientele and can cost a lot, but there are a growing number of smaller, less expensive places, especially for lunch.

On the whole, the Swedes eat earlier than other nations. Lunch is served from 11:00 A.M., the evening meal usually at 6:00 P.M. Bigger restaurants, city hotels, and motels expect their guests to arrive later, and many cafés and dance restaurants serve food well into the night.

For a typically Swedish offering, try one of the many *korvkiosk* along the city streets. These covered food stalls serve plain but good fare: sausage (which is what *korv* means), grilled chicken, and, nowadays, the inevitable hamburgers and chips. While in Stockholm, pay a visit to the *Saluhall,* an atmospheric food hall on Östermalmstorg, where delicatessen stalls selling meat, cheese, fish, and cakes are complemented by a number of good cafés and restaurants.

Note: Some restaurants will charge a fee of 5–10 Skr for leaving your coat in the cloak room, which you are obliged to do anyway.

What to Eat

Hotel **breakfasts** (*frukost*) are a less lavish version of the *smörgåsbord* cold table (see page 100), but are still enough to keep anyone going for most of the day. The *dagens rätt* **lunch** menu is also good value.

The Crayfish and "Sour Herring" Season (*Kräft och Surströmmingspremiären*)

Swedes have an understandable passion for crayfish and —to those not born to it—an inexplicable addiction to *surströmming* (fermented herring), which replaces crayfish further north.

The crayfish season starts in August with a grand party, indoors or out. Sporting comic hats and paper bibs, guests sit at a long table lit by paper lanterns and loaded with glasses, aquavit, and delicious crayfish. Eating is punctuated by toasts, traditional songs, and toasting songs, including the best known of all, *Helan går* ... (something equivalent to "down it in one"), the intricacies of which are better attempted than explained.

Surströmming is a dish made of Baltic herring, salted and set aside for a long time, then put into sealed tins. With the herring, the brave eat *tunnbröd* (thin bread), raw onions, and *mandelpotatis* (small, sweetish, almond-shaped potatoes). Connoisseurs claim that milk is the correct drink.

To many Swedes—and all foreigners—the downing of this overpowering meal is virtually a test of machismo.

The Swedes like the natural products of river and forest, particularly fish (a speciality in Gothenburg) and meats such as venison and reindeer. Foods typical of midsummer are herring and boiled new potatoes flavoured with dill (a popular herb) followed by a heap of fresh strawberries.

Old-fashioned ice cream cones served up just as you like them in Gamla Stan.

One dish that you may like to try is *gravad lax* (delicately marinaded salmon) —many people find this preferable to smoked salmon. It is always served with a dill sauce. The ubiquitous boiled potatoes arrive with most meals, also sprinkled with dill.

Fiskbullar (fish balls) are also popular, as are *köttbullar* (meatballs). Two typically Swedish dishes which hark back to the days when nothing was allowed to go to waste, are *Janssons Frestelse* (Jansson's Temptation), a tangy mixture of potato, onion, and anchovy, and *pyttipana* (literally, "put in the pan"), a delicious hodgepodge of leftovers all fried up together. In many rural areas of Sweden you can still enjoy these traditional dishes, which are known by the general term *husmanskost* (home cooking).

There is also a selection of delicious buns (*bullar*)—at their best in the baker's shop at Skansen. *Semlor,* once a traditional Shrove Tuesday delight eaten before the long fast, is now popular enough to appear immediately after Christmas. With a filling of almond paste and whipped cream, the buns are correctly served in a dish of hot milk with a sprinkling of cinnamon.

Våfflor (waffles), thought by many to be North American, were in fact introduced there by Scandinavian emigrants. In their original homeland they are simply mouth-watering.

If you're visiting Småland and "The Glass Country" (see page 49), look out for **Hyttsill Evenings.** These continue an old tradition from times when the glassblowing hall was a social as well as a work place for local people, who cooked herring beside the furnaces. The pudding that follows is the traditional Småland delicacy, curd cake with sour cherry or strawberry jam, eaten in the glow of the furnace to the sound of traditional music and story-telling.

Fruits of the Forest

The country's forests provide mushrooms (*svamp*) and wild berries, which *allemansrätt* (see page 110) allows you to pick anywhere; it is almost fashionable to return with stained fingers after a summer weekend. A profuse variety of wild berries grows in Scandinavia, from *smultron* (wild strawberries) to *hjortron* (cloudberries)—causing endless confusion, as different countries all have their own names for the different types.

Smörgåsbord

It is a tribute to the rise of Swedish cuisine that people all over the world can say the word *smörgåsbord,* the great cold-table buffet common to all three Scandinavian nations.

The *smörgåsbord* is a substantial, celebratory meal that's served on Sundays and special occasions. It has also begun to appear on hotel menus as something typically Swedish.

It starts with herring of various sorts, shrimp, salmon, and other fish. Next come the cold meats and cheeses, with caviar, eggs, and different salads. This is followed by hot dishes, even though it is a "cold" table, with fruit or pudding and coffee to follow. The farming area of Skåne in the south, as guardian of

the old way of life, claims to make the best *smörgåsbord.*
Hotel breakfasts are a smaller version of the meal.

Drinks

To drink with a meal, there are three strengths of beer: light
(Class I), ordinary (Class II), and export (Class III). You can
purchase wine for not much more than 35 Skr in the state alcohol stores, *Systembolaget,* but restaurants multiply that by
three or more in an effort, so some say, to keep beer and spirit prices more reasonable. Aquavit is a must with herring at
the start of the *smörgåsbord.*

Aquavit

Most European countries have their own favourite firewater;
in Scandinavia it is Aquavit (*Akvavit*)—the water of life —
which is also sometimes called *snaps.* Sweden's most popular brand is *Skåne.*

Straight aquavit is distilled from potatoes or barley. What
makes each brand different is what goes into it afterwards—
juniper, coriander, or perhaps myrtle, or whatever distinctive
flavour the distiller can devise.

Aquavit is served in tiny glasses and quaffed ice cold
(many families cool it in the freezer rather than the fridge, or
in the snow outside at a winter *stuga*). It is drunk at the beginning of a meal, usually as an accompaniment to fish—
ideally the herring that starts a *smörgåsbord.* Raising your
glass in a toast is an essential part of the ancient ritual of
drinking aquavit.

Many experiment with their own flavours, putting a leaf or
sprig of herbs into a half bottle and leaving it to mature.
Some make their own, so if you're offered a selection of
aquavit in a private house, don't enquire about the brand.
Home distilling is an open secret.

To Help You Order ...

May I have the menu, please. **Kan jag få matsedeln, tack.**
What do you recommend? **Vad rekommenderar ni?**
Do you have any vegetarian **Har ni några vegetariska**
  dishes? **rätter?**
I'd like to pay. **Får jag betala.**

beetroot	**rödbetor**	prawns	**räkor**
carrots	**morötter**	reindeer	**ren**
cauliflower	**blomkål**	roast beef	**rostbiff**
chicken	**kyckling**	roast lamb	**lammstek**
egg dishes	**äggrätter**	salmon	**lax**
ham	**skinka**	smoked Baltic	
mushrooms	**svamp**	herring	**böckling**
octopus	**bläckfisk**	spinach	**spenat**
onions	**lök**	tomatoes	**tomater**
peas	**ärtor**	trout	**forell**
pike	**gädda**	tuna	**tonfisk**
pork chop	**fläskkotlett**	venison	**rådjur**

... and Read the Menu

bakverk	pastries	**ost**	cheese
drycker	drinks	**pasterätter**	pasta
efterrätter	desserts	**risrätter**	rice
fisk	fish	**sallader**	salad
frukt	fruit	**skaldjur**	seafood
från grillen	grilled (broiled)	**soppor**	soups
fågel	poultry	**smårätter**	snacks
förrätter	first course	**smörgåsar**	sandwiches
glass	ice-cream	**smörgåsbord**	cold table
grönsaker	vegetables	**varmrätter**	main course
huvudrätter	main course	**vilt**	game
kött	meat	**vinlista**	wine list

INDEX

HANDY TRAVEL TIPS

An A–Z Summary of Practical Information

A

ACCOMMODATION *(logi)*

(See also CAMPING, YOUTH HOSTELS, and the list of RECOMMENDED HOTELS starting on page 129)

Swedish hotels *(hotell)* are almost invariably warm, comfortable, and well run. Many higher-grade hotels have saunas and plunge pools and some also have swimming pools. They are also among Europe's higher-priced hotels, and the secret to keeping costs reasonable is to choose the time you visit Sweden. Hotels are geared to business travel and during slack periods (early summer to mid- or late-August and at weekends) they slash their rates (sometimes by as much as 50%). Always ask about discounts and special rates, including the special Stockholm, Gothenburg, and Malmö packages. In addition, many Swedish hotel chains offer special rates, usually in summer. Sweden Hotels, for instance, has a "Scandinavian Bonuspass" which carries 15–50% discounts (usually May through September and winter weekends) at their hotels throughout the country. (It also has a reciprocal scheme with hotels in Norway, Denmark, and Finland.) Svenska Turistförening hotels (see page 128) also offer good value.

Before making plans—and certainly bookings—ask for a copy of the Swedish Travel Board's Council's excellent *Hotels in Sweden* booklet, which lists hotels and gives details of all schemes.

Self-catering accommodation is also good. A Swedish family may rent out its own *stuga* (traditional wooden holiday house). Tour operators and tourist offices offer self-catering packages and there are more than 350 purpose-built holiday villages, with canoes, bikes, boats, etc. for hire.

AIRPORTS *(flygplatser)*

Sweden's three main airports are Arlanda (serving Stockholm and Uppsala), Landvetter (Gothenburg), and Sturup (Malmö), the last mainly for internal flights. All have airport coaches to and from their respective city's Central Station. Taxis are more expensive. SAS operates a limousine service to any address in the surrounding area, which is costly for a single passenger but less so if sharing.

Arlanda has four terminals, three domestic and one overseas, with inter-terminal buses. There are self-service cafés, a restaurant, duty-free, and Swedish food shops, a hotel, a tourist/accommodation office, and car-hire desks. Arlanda is 42 km (26 miles) from the centre of Stockholm. The airport bus stops at Brommaplan (western suburbs), Ulriksdal (northern suburbs), Skt Eriksplan (inner city), and Terminalen at Central Station, where there is a taxi-rank for onward journeys. There are also special bus and taxi offers to and from hotels. Arlanda tel. (0) 8-797-60-00.

Landvetter is smaller, with a good, small hotel, duty-free shop, and self-service restaurant. Situated 24 km (17 miles) from Gothenburg, there is an airport bus which takes around 30 minutes to and from the centre. Landvetter tel. (031) 94-11-00.

Malmö-Sturup is 30 km (21 miles) from the city centre (roughly 40 minutes). It has one terminal with a restaurant, cafés, and duty-free shop, and there is an airport hotel. Sturup tel. (040) 613-11-00.

B

BICYCLE HIRE/RENTAL

Sweden's uncrowded roads make cycling popular, and bicycles can be rented almost anywhere; the local tourist office usually has details. Typical cost: 110 Skr per day. Further details from: Svenska Turistföreningen, Box 25, S-101-20 Stockholm; tel. (08) 463-22-00, and Cykelfrämjandet, Box 6027, S-102-31; tel. (08) 32-16-80, which publishes a *"Swedish Cycling"* guide in English.

BUDGETING for YOUR TRIP

All prices given are approximate. In this large country, different areas have different prices, and Stockholm is usually the most expensive.

Car hire: Prices vary considerably. All quotes are for unlimited mileage. A small car (Ford Escort) for the weekend: 1,135 Skr; for the week: 2,255 Skr. A large car (Volvo 540): for the wekend, 1,369 Skr; for the week, 2,700 Skr.

Guides: Guides are not cheap: around 750 Skr for three hours, and 250 Skr or more for each additional hour, plus booking fee of 150 Skr.

Hotels: Average rates for hotels (per night) can be divided into three categories (based on two people sharing a double room and including full breakfast): under 1,100 Skr; 1,100–1,800 Skr; over 1,800 Skr. Prices at the lower end may be well below 1,100 Skr, but equally, prices at the top end may rise considerably above 1,800 Skr. These are full rates. Visitors can take advantage of weekend, special, and summer rates and packages. (See also ACCOMMODATION and the list of RECOMMENDED HOTELS starting on page 129)

Meals and drinks. Continental breakfast in a restaurant/café costs 40–70 Skr; lunch 50–70 Skr; dinner at a medium-priced restaurant (not including drinks) 200 Skr per head; coffee or soft drinks 15 Skr; bottle of wine 150 Skr and up; spirits (4cl) 70 Skr, except aquavit (4cl) 50 Skr. Like hotel breakfasts, lunch can be a good bet. Look for the sign *Dagens rätt* (dish of the day): salad, a main course, and coffee. Food and (especially) alcoholic drink are expensive. Self-caterers are advised to bring in a car-load of food and other necessities.

Museums: 20–80 Skr, average 30 Skr. (Some are free.)

Petrol costs 8 Skr per litre and diesel about 5.75 Skr. Many petrol stations have automatic 24-hour pumps, which take 100 Skr notes.

Public transport: Costs vary from place to place, but in Stockholm a single ticket for bus/*Tunnelbana*/local train is 14 Skr.

Stockholm Tourist Card: Unlimited free travel on *Tunnelbana* and buses but no sightseeing concessions. Cost: 60 Skr for 24 hours for journeys within the Greater Stockholm area (36 Skr for under-18s); three-day ticket 120 Skr. Similar concessionary travel tickets are sold at *Pressbyrån* (newspaper shops). Note: travel on Stockholm's buses is free for one parent if you have one or more children in a stroller.

Sweden

Taxis: Basic charge 45–80 Skr within the city area. Some Stockholm taxis have a set fare of 85 Skr within the Stockholm city boundaries.

Tourist City Cards: Stockholm, Gothenburg, and Malmö all have concessionary cards, with big savings on sightseeing, public transport, and shopping, bought from tourist information centres.

Stockholmskort (Stockholm Card) gives free travel for one adult and 3 children (under 18) on local transport services (except airport), free city parking, sightseeing by coach and boat, and entry to many places of interest. A basic 24-hour card costs 199 Skr, and a 72-hour card 498 Skr. Gothenburg and Malmö have similar schemes.

All three cities offer **packages** which include accommodation at selected hotels, plus a "Kort" (discount card), available mid-June to mid-August and at weekends throughout the year.

Trains: Single journey between Stockholm and Gothenburg, second class 430 Skr. Single sleeper journey, Stockholm–Kiruna second class, rail ticket 505 Skr plus sleeper 790, depending on the facilities available (see also page 124).

Video: To rent a video camera 400 Skr for 24 hours, 450 Skr a weekend, plus *MOMS*. Cost of a 3-hour cassette tape 50 Skr.

C

CAMPING (*camping*)

There are 750 graded camping sites, often by lake or sea, with boats, canoes, and bikes for hire, and maybe riding, mini-golf, and tennis on offer. Most are open in June–August, some earlier but not necessarily with full facilities. Around 200 sites open in winter-sports areas.

You must have a Camping Card to use Swedish campsites, available for around 49 Skr at the first campsite at which you stay, but not required if you hold an International Camping Card. Note: Only propane gas (eg. Primus) is allowed in Sweden, *never* butane.

Sweden's access tradition, *allemansrätt* (Everyone's Right) allows you one-night's camping anywhere, without permission (even on private property), but campers should not stay too close to houses, damage their surroundings, or leave litter. Instead of tents or caravans many sites have 2- to 6-bed log cabins equipped with cooking facilities and utensils, but not bedding (bring sleeping bags).

Further details are available in the brochure *Camping in Sweden*, available from the Swedish Travel Council (see page 123).

CAR HIRE/RENTAL *(biluthyrning)*
(See also DRIVING and MONEY MATTERS)

Most big companies, such as Avis, Hertz, Budget, and Europcar have offices in airports and larger towns, with a wide range of cars. Special rates are usually available between mid-June and mid-August, and weekends throughout the year. Always ask about discounts, particularly packages connected with domestic air and rail travel. You can often rent a car in one place and return it to another.

Most companies ask for a **deposit,** which is usually a credit card imprint. The legal minimum **driving age** in Sweden is 18, but to hire a car you usually need to have held a licence for three years, so in practice the minimum age is **21.** Check up on **Collision Damage Reducer** (not "Waiver" as in other countries), which costs around 70 Skr a day and limits damage liability to 500 Skr.

CLIMATE and CLOTHING

Most of Sweden has a continental climate with a medium to large temperature difference between summer and winter. Shorts and T-shirts are often the norm in Stockholm during the summer, when everyone swims. Temperatures above 20°C (70°F) are not unusual.

The climate can be particularly variable in the west, which has more rain than inland or eastern Sweden. Long hours of sunlight can mean high temperatures in the north, and swimsuit skiing on the northern border at Björkliden, near Riksgränsen, is not unknown. Conversely, in the depth of winter, temperatures in the north can sink as low as -30°C (-22°F).

The brief northern spring turns swiftly to summer around the end of May, but by the end of September autumn is turning into winter. The seasons in the south are more even. Autumn, with light frost at night and the glowing sun on the changing colours of the foliage by day, is beautiful. From Gothenburg to Malmö the west coast climate is moderated by an open sea which rarely freezes.

The chart below shows the average daily maximum and minimum temperatures and number of rainy days each month in Stockholm.

	J	F	M	A	M	J	J	A	S	O	N	D
Max °F	31	31	37	45	57	65	70	66	58	48	38	33
Max °C	-1	-1	3	7	14	18	21	19	14	9	3	1
Min °F	23	22	26	32	41	49	55	53	46	39	31	26
Min °C	-5	-6	-3	0	5	9	13	12	8	4	-1	-3
Days of rainfall	10	7	6	7	7	8	9	10	9	9	10	11

Clothing. It is a good idea to be prepared for changes and to wear several layers. Even in summer keep a sweater and waterproof covering to hand, as well as T-shirts, shorts or a skirt, and cotton trousers. The north always demands warm outerwear.

Winter also calls for layers. Houses are warm and the custom is to leave heavy clothing just inside the front door (or in your hotel cloakroom). Walkers should take good walking boots and a rucksack. Winter essentials are headgear, preferably wool or fur, and two pairs of gloves or mitts (one thin, one thick). Good footwear is necessary for snow and slushy streets. If you plan to be out of doors a lot, a thermal layer is advised. For evenings, Swedes dress informally, casual but smart.

COMMUNICATIONS

Post offices (*postkontor*). Swedish postboxes are yellow. Post offices usually open 9am–6pm Monday through Friday, 10am–2pm Saturday. Some branches close on Saturday in July.

Telephones (*telefon*) **and faxes.** Swedish post offices do not have telephones but there are plenty of payphones in stations, streets, hotels, and other public institutions, as well as special Telegraph Offices (marked *Telia*) which also send faxes. (Most hotels should be able to send faxes as well.) Automatic payphones are always cheaper than those in hotels. Credit-card phones (indicated by a CCC sign) are also plentiful. Calls within Europe cost around 3–6 Skr a minute.

COMPLAINTS

The Swedish sense of fair play makes complaining a rare event. In a restaurant or hotel, a quiet word with the manager is usually enough. Serious complaints about hotels or other major services should be directed to tourist offices or to the appropriate travel authority.

CRIME (See also EMERGENCIES and POLICE)

Sweden is one of the safest countries in the world. It is safe to walk in cities at night, but on Friday and Saturday evenings you may meet groups of revellers—who are likely to be noisy rather than dangerous—and Stockholm's *Tunnelbana* (underground) can be boisterous. You may prefer a taxi. Should anything happen to you, contact the police. The emergency number **112** is free when called from payphones.

CUSTOMS and ENTRY FORMALITIES

Europeans and North Americans need only a valid passport to enter Sweden. Visitors from the U.K. need only a British Visitor's Passport. Other nationalities should check with local Swedish Consulates.

Duty-free. Allowances into **Sweden** are as follows: for residents of European countries 200 cigarettes or 50 cigars or 250g tobacco, 1l of wine and 1l of spirits; for residents of non-European countries 400 cigarettes or 100 cigars or 500g tobacco, 1l wine and 1l spirits. When returning to your own country you may take the following: **Australia:** 250 cigarettes or 250g tobacco, 1l wine or spirits; **Canada:** 200 cigarettes and 50 cigars and 400g tobacco, 1.1l wine or spirits or 8.5l beer; **New Zealand:** 200 cigarettes or 50 cigars or 250g tobacco, 4.5l wine or beer and 1.1l spirits; **Republic of Ireland:** 200 cigarettes or 50 cigars or 250g tobacco, 2l wine or 1l spirits; **South Africa:** 400 cigarettes and 50 cigars and 250g tobacco, 2l wine and 1l spirits; **U.K.:** 200 cigarettes or 50 cigars or 250g tobacco, 2l still wine and 1l spirits; **U.S.A.:** 200 cigarettes and 100 cigars and 2kg tobacco, 1l wine or spirits.

Currency restrictions. There is no restriction on the amount you can take into or out of Sweden.

D

DRIVING IN SWEDEN

Swedish roads are well-maintained and uncrowded; outside the cities driving is easy, despite the small number of motorways.

Speed limits. Speed limits, shown on road signs, are usually 50 km/h (30 mph) in built-up areas; 70 km/h (43 mph) on trunk roads and 90 or 110 km/h (55 or 70 mph) on motorways. Caravan limits are lower.

Documents. To drive your own car in Sweden you need: a national or international driving licence; car registration documents; green card or other valid third party (or comprehensive) insurance.

Driving rules. Drive on the right, pass on the left, and, unless road signs indicate otherwise, give way to traffic approaching from the right. Traffic on a roundabout usually has right of way. Seatbelts are obligatory for everyone in the car. Dipped headlights (which should be adjusted on right-hand-drive cars) must be used both day and night.

Drunk-driving laws are strict and well enforced. Drinking when in charge of a car attracts very high fines, or even a jail sentence. The best course is never to drink if you're driving. In the effort to stamp out drinking and driving, police carry out fairly frequent spot checks on licences and vehicles.

Accidents and breakdowns. Contact either the local police or *Larmtjänst*, run by Swedish insurance companies, which operates a 24-hour recovery service. Telephone numbers are listed in Swedish telephone directories.

Serious accidents, especially if there are injuries, warrant use of the **112** emergency number for the police. Although it is not mandatory to call the police to an accident, even if damage is slight drivers must give their name and contact address to others involved before leaving the scene. Drivers who do not stop after an accident are liable to a fine or, in certain cases, imprisonment.

International pictographs are widely used, although you may see some signs in Swedish.

Biljettautomat	ticket machine
Bussfil	bus lane
Busshållplats	bus stop
Ej genomfart	no through traffic
Privat parkering	private parking
Körkort	driving licence

Other Useful Vocabulary:

Car registration papers	**besiktningsinstrument**
Please check the oil/tyres/battery.	**Kan ni kontrollera oljan/däcken/batteriet, tack.**
I've broken down.	**Bilen har gått sönder.**
There's been an accident.	**Det har hänt en olycka.**

Fluid measures

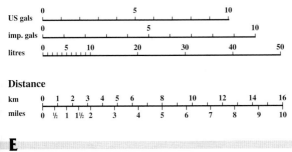

Distance

E

ELECTRIC CURRENT

Swedish electricity is 220 volts AC, and requires standard two-pin, round continental plugs. Visitors should bring their own adapters.

Sweden

EMBASSIES and CONSULATES *(ambassad; konsulat)*

Britain: Skapögatan 6-8, Box 27819, S-155-93 Stockholm;
tel. (08) 671-90-00, fax (08) 671-91-00.

Ireland: Östermalmsgatan 97, Box 103-26, S-100-55 Stockholm;
tel. (08) 661-80-05.

U.S.A.: Strandvägen 101, 115-89 Stockholm; tel. (08) 783-53-00.

Most embassies are open 8am–4pm, but there is usually someone on
duty 24 hours a day. Telephone in advance if in doubt.

EMERGENCIES (See also POLICE)

Radio Sweden broadcasts vital messages to travellers in Sweden on
medium wave 1179KHz (254m) and in the Stockholm area on FM
89.6MHz. Messages should be sent to a broadcasting organization in
your country of origin, Interpol, or the appropriate embassy in Sweden (see EMBASSIES AND CONSULATES and MEDIA).

For the **police, fire brigade,** or **ambulance,** dial **112** from anywhere in Sweden. Calls are free from pay phones.

ETIQUETTE (See also TIPPING)

The most useful word is *tack* (thank you), which is used very often,
partly because there is no precise equivalent for "please" in Swedish.
Swedes are punctual and the idea of "7:30 for 8" does not exist.
When drinks are served, it is polite to wait for the host/hostess to
raise the glass with a *Skål!* (Cheers!) or *Välkommen och Skål!* (Welcome and Skål!). Eye contact is important, both with your glass
raised for *Skål* and immediately after the first taste.

If invited to a private house, it is customary to take flowers to your
hostess and, to be quite correct, to phone the following day to say
Tack för senast (literally, "thanks for last time").

In contrast, all Scandinavians have a relaxed attitude to nudity,
particularly in the sauna (*bastu*). Even so, men and women usually
use the *bastu* separately (unless with family or close friends), perhaps meeting afterwards in their bathrobes to cool off with a beer.

If you're travelling with children, note that spanking or smacking children is now illegal in Sweden, and if you do so in public you are likely to come up against indignant law-abiding citizens.

G

GAY and LESBIAN TRAVELLERS

Sweden is one of the world's most progressive countries when it comes to gay rights. Since 1988 government legislation has granted gay relationships the same status as heterosexual marriages and the state has given financial support to gay organizations. Information and advice can be obtained from the Swedish Federation for Lesbian and Gay Rights: RSFL (*Riksförbundet för Sexuellt Likaberättigade*), Stockholms Gay-hus, Sveavägen 57. (Postal address: Förbund-skansli, Box 350, S-101-26 Stockholm); tel. (08) 736-02-13.

GUIDES *(guide)* and TOURS

English is Sweden's second language, which makes it easy to get an English-speaking guide. German-speaking guides are almost as plentiful. Bus or boat tours are multi-lingual, as are those in some museums and other places of interest. Local tourist offices can also make bookings for tours and guides, or tell you where to book. In Stockholm authorized guides can be booked by ringing (08) 789-24-31 or (08) 789-24-90.

L

LANGUAGE

School children learn English from the age of nine, and most Swedes speak excellent English, a little less so in remote areas. German is the next choice of language and is spoken by many (particularly in the tourist industry). City menus often give English translations.

The word *turist* (as in *Abisko Turiststation*) in Swedish means "tourist" in the Scandinavian sense of someone who travels in remote areas under his or her own power, not "tourist" as in English.

117

Sweden

Swedish is not easy to pronounce and the language has three extra vowels: å, ä, and ö (listed as the last three letters of the alphabet).

Useful Expressions

big/small	**stor/liten**	next/last	**nästa/sista**
quick/slow	**snabb/långsam**	good/bad	**bra/dålig**
hot/cold	**varm/kall**	early/late	**tidig/sen**
heavy/light	**tung/lätt**	cheap/expensive	**billig/dyr**
open/shut	**öpen/stängd**	near/far	**nära/långt (bort)**
right/wrong	**rätt/fel**		
old/new	**gammal/ny**	here/there	**här/där**

Days of the Week

Sunday	**söndag**	Thursday	**torsdag**
Monday	**måndag**	Friday	**fredag**
Tuesday	**tisdag**	Saturday	**lördag**
Wednesday	**onsdag**		

Months

January	**januari**	July	**juli**
February	**februari**	August	**augusti**
March	**mars**	September	**september**
April	**april**	October	**oktober**
May	**maj**	November	**november**
June	**juni**	December	**december**

*The names of days and months aren't capitalized in Swedish.

LOST PROPERTY *(hittegods)*

Stockholm: Main Lost Property Office *(hittegodsexpedition)*; tel. (0) 8-401-00-00
Stockholm Local Traffic Office (SL); tel. (0) 8-736-07-80, for property lost on buses, *Tunnelbana* and local trains.

Gothenburg: Railway Lost Property, tel. (031) 10-44-66
Police Lost Property, tel. (031) 700-46-00
Public Transport Lost Property, tel. (031) 80-20-88

Malmö: Lost Property; tel. (0) 40-20-10-00

If you lose property elsewhere, first retrace your steps and then try the main police, railway, or bus station.

M

MEDIA

Radio and television. *Sveriges Radio* (Radio Sweden) and *Sveriges Television* (Swedish Television) are the main companies, though there are now also local radio and various commercial television channels. *Sveriges Radio* broadcasts regular 30-minute programmes of news and information in English, which can be heard over most of Sweden on medium wave 1179KHz (254m), and also in the Stockholm area on FM 89.6MHz. Further details are available from Radio Sweden International, S-105-10 Stockholm; tel. (08) 784-50-00, fax (08) 667-62-83, or from many hotels. Gothenburg local radio also has a daily half-hour English news and tourist information programme. In addition to Swedish channels, most hotels carry English-language satellite channels such as Super Channel and CNN, plus German-language channels direct from Germany.

Newspapers and magazines (*tidning; tidskrift*). Sweden's main daily newspapers are *Svenska Dagbladet, Dagens Nyheter,* and *Göteborgs Posten* (broadsheets), and *Expressen* and *Aftonbladet* (tabloids), all in Swedish. English-language newspapers are on sale in kiosks and central stations. Stockholm's Kulturhuset (Culture House) has a selection of English-language newspapers to read on the premises, as do the City Libraries in Stockholm and Gothenburg. Stockholm also has a visitors' newspaper, *Stockholm this Week*, and Malmö has *Malmö this Month*.

MEDICAL CARE (See also EMERGENCIES)

No vaccinations are needed for Sweden, nor does the country have the equivalent of the general-practice surgery.

If you become ill, ask your hotel to call a doctor who is affiliated to *Försäkringskassan* (Swedish National Health Service). If you are

Sweden

able, go to the casualty department, *Akutmottagning*, at a hospital, or *Vårdcentral* (health centre) in more rural areas. Take your passport with you for identification. Hospital visits cost 120 Skr (230 Skr for the casualty department). Take a doctor's prescription for medicines to any chemist (*apotek*). These are open during shopping hours.

All-night chemists can be found in the following places:

Stockholm: CW Scheele, Klarabergsgatan 64; tel. (08) 454-81-30

Gothenburg: Vasen, Götgatan 12; tel. (0) 31-80-44-10

Malmö: Gripen, Bergsgatan 48; tel. (0) 40-19-21-10

Dental treatment. *Tandläkare* means dental surgery. Emergency services in larger cities are shown on health "blue" pages of the business telephone directory. Sweden has a reciprocal agreement for medical treatment with Britain and most European countries, which means citizens of those countries are entitled to the same emergency service as Swedes.

MONEY MATTERS

Currency. Swedish currency is the *krona* (or crown, plural *kronor*), made up of 100 *öre*. It is abbreviated kr, Skr, or SEK (banker's abbreviation). Coins come in 50 öre, 1 krona, and 5 and 10 kronor. Bank notes are 20, 50, 100, and 1,000 kronor.

Exchange facilities. You can change currency at: airports; the Central Stations in Malmö, Stockholm, and Gothenburg; almost all commercial and savings banks; post offices; branches of "Forex" (bureaux de change); hotels; and some department stores.

Credit cards. Most well-known credit cards are accepted. Shops and restaurants usually indicate which they take. Individual banks often have links to particular cards for currency exchange facilities.

Traveller's cheques. Banks and hotels will change traveller's cheques or cash, but banks usually give a better rate. Shops accept traveller's cheques for purchases.

O

OPENING HOURS (See also PUBLIC HOLIDAYS)

Shops: Weekday opening 9am–6pm; weekends 1pm–4pm. Some big stores and shopping centres in larger towns stay open until 8 or 10pm. In rural areas, closing times for shops and petrol stations is usually 5 or 6pm. Shops close early the day before a public holiday.

Banks: 9:30am–3pm; in larger cities some stay open until 5:30pm. Banks close on Saturday except for those at airports: Arlanda Airport daily 6:30am–9pm; Landvetter Airport Monday through Friday 9am–4pm; Sturup Airport daily 8am–8pm.

P

PHOTOGRAPHY (*fotografering*)

You can buy most makes of cameras in Sweden, including the superb Swedish Hasselblad brand. Colour films usually take three or four days to be developed, but in the cities many shops offer same-day or next-day services.

I'd like a film for this camera.	**Jag skulle vilja ha en film till den här kameran.**
black and white film	**svartvit film**
colour prints	**färgfilm**
colour slides	**färgfilm för diabilder**
How long will it take to develop (and print) this film?	**Hur lång tid tar det att framkalla (och göra kopior av) den här filmen?**

POLICE (*polis*) (See also EMERGENCIES)

Main Police stations are open 24 hours and have a public desk for incidents, thefts, or other problems, and usually a local lost property office. Police patrols tour the streets and random car checks are more frequent than in many other countries.

Sweden

The emergency police number (also fire, ambulance, etc.) is **112;** no money is required from a pay phone.

PUBLIC HOLIDAYS *(helgdag)* (See also OPENING HOURS)

Banks, shops, and offices close on the public holidays listed below, and may also close earlier the day before. Cinemas, museums, and restaurants may stay open on public holidays. The country grinds to a standstill on 24 December, the day Swedes celebrate Christmas.

Near Year's Day	*Nyårsdagen*	1 January
Twelfth Night	*Trettondagen*	6 January
Labour Day	*Första Maj*	1 May
Midsummer Day	*Midsommarsdagen*	Sat between 21 and 26 June
All Saints' Day	*Allhelgondagen*	Sat between 31 Oct and 6 Nov
Christmas Eve	*Julafton*	24 December
Christmas Day	*Juldagen*	25 December
Boxing Day	*Annandag jul*	26 December

Movable Dates:

Good Friday	*Långfredagen*	late March/early April
Easter/Easter Monday	*Annandagpåsk*	late March/early April
Ascension Day	*Kristi himmelfårdsdagen*	May
Whit Monday	*Annandag pingst*	May

R

RELIGION

Around 95 percent of native Swedes are Lutheran, but there are also over 60,000 Roman Catholics, plus Jewish and other faiths. Numbers of Muslims have grown with immigration, but still account for only a small proportion of the population. Lutheran and other churches are listed in telephone directories and *Malmö This Month*.

TIME DIFFERENCES

Sweden keeps Central European Time, one hour ahead of Greenwich Mean Time. Clocks go forward by one hour during the summer (late March to late September). This differs in duration from British Summer Time and can cause some confusion with airline schedules, etc.

New York	London	Paris	**Stockholm**	Sydney	Auckland
6am	11am	noon	**noon**	8pm	10pm

TIPPING

Egalitarian Sweden is not a tipping nation. Service charges are included in bills, but it is usual to round up the restaurant bill to the nearest 10 Skr. It is not necessary to leave a tip for the chambermaid.

Taxi drivers do not normally expect a tip, but it is customary to round up the fare to the nearest 10 Skr. Add 10 percent if, for example, the driver carries a case up a flight of stairs. When you leave a coat in a cloakroom, the charge is usually 7 Skr per article.

TOURIST INFORMATION OFFICES

Sweden is divided into 24 regional tourist organizations, and there are some 300 tourist offices in total. All have a selection of brochures, leaflets, and maps of their respective areas.

The Sweden Travel Shop occupies the same building as the Stockholm Information Centre (Sweden House) and has a wide selection of information on regions other than Stockholm, plus a similar advice and booking service. On the upper floors in Sweden House are the Swedish Institute's library and its excellent bookshop.

Tourist offices (*turistbyråer*) are marked with the international tourist sign (white "i" on green background) and in season are very busy. The staff answer questions, help with (and book) accommodation and tours, and often have typical Swedish goods on sale.

Sweden

Stockholm Information Service (including other sections in Sweden House), Sverigehuset, Kungsträdgården, Box 7542, S-103-93 Stockholm; tel. (08) 789-24-90

Gothenburg Tourist Office, Kungsportsplatsen 2, S-411-10 Göteborg; tel. (031) 10-07-40

Malmö Tourist Office, Skeppsbron 2, S-211-20 Malmö; tel. (040) 30-01-50

Swedish Travel and Tourism Council, Kungsgatan 36, Box 3030, S-103-61 Stockholm; tel. (08) 725-55-00; fax (08) 725-55-31

Overseas Offices

Great Britain: Swedish Travel & Tourism Council, 11 Montagu Place, London W1HZAL; tel. (0171) 274-58-68

U.S.A.: Swedish Tourist Board, 655 Third Avenue, 18th floor, New York NY 10017; tel. 212-885-9700

TRANSPORT

Sweden has good and well-maintained bus and rail services. Long distances make domestic airlines important. Cities and larger towns are linked by SAS and Braathen Airlines.

Buses (*bussar*). Swebus and Svenska Buss operate express bus services between larger towns in Southern and Central Sweden and between Stockholm and the northern coastal towns. There are also weekend-only services on main routes. A postal bus network operates in the north.

In cities bus service is frequent, comprehensive, and well integrated with other transport. Stockholm's bus network is the largest in the world, run by the Stockholm Transit Authority, which also operates integrated underground and local train services. Gothenburg has an ecologically friendly tram network.

Trains (*tåg*). The network run by Swedish State Railways (SJ) covers the whole country, with new X2000 high-speed trains cutting times on Stockholm–Gothenburg and Stockholm–Karlstad trips.

Long-distance trains have restaurant cars and/or buffets, and there are also sleepers and couchettes for both first and second class.

The *reslustkort* (wanderlust card) offers half-price, second-class travel on certain trains, and other cost-cutting benefits. It is valid for one year, costs 150 Skr, and is good value. On some trains, marked "R" or "IC," you must reserve a seat (price 20 Skr), which can be done right up to the time of departure.

Inlandsbanan (Inland Railway), a special scenic line, runs from Mora, in Dalarna, to Gällivare beyond the Arctic Circle. *Wildmarksexpressen* (the Wilderness Express) has old 1930s coaches with a gourmet restaurant, and runs on the same line between Östersund and Gällivare, with stops and excursions (see page 77). Further details are available from Inlandståget AB, Kyrkagatan 56, S-831-34 Östersund; tel. (063) 12-76-90.

Full-fare tickets can be bought outside Sweden free of VAT, which is charged on tickets bought in Sweden. Ask at travel agents.

Taxis (*taxi*). Taxi ranks are marked *taxi*, but you can also hail taxis on the street. A lit sign, *Ledig*, means a taxi is free. You can also book by phone: look under *Gula Sidorna* in the telephone directory for numbers. Taxis have meters and willingly issue receipts; overcharging is not usually a problem.

Underground (*tunnelbana*). Stockholm Transit Authority runs the underground, *Tunnelbana* or *T-banan*, which covers 95 km (60 miles) of track and incorporates 100 stations. These are marked with a large "T," are very clean, and have been nicknamed the "world's largest art exhibition," because of specially commissioned artwork in many of them. Stockholm also runs a good system of local trains.

Ferries and boats (*färja; båt*). Despite its many waterways and large lakes, more often ferries connect Sweden to other countries rather than linking it internally. Many islands have regular connections, one of the busiest ports being the Baltic island of Gotland (see page 52). There are also tourist boats in and around the Stockholm archipelago and in other coastal areas, in addition to regular services.

Sweden

Big lakes, such as Vänern, Vättern, Mälaren, Siljan, Storsjön, and others, also have services.

The Göta Canal (see page 62) is a classic pleasure route for Swedes and visitors alike. Details of canal trips are available from Rederi AB Göta Kanal, Hotellplatsen 2, Box 272, S-401-24 Göteborg; tel. (031) 80-63-15, fax (031) 15-83-11.

TRAVELLERS with DISABILITIES

Facilities for disabled people include access ramps, lifts, and hotel rooms adapted for people with mobility difficulties or allergies, good public transport access, and special provisions for swimming and riding. Almost all pedestrian crossings use sound to indicate when it is safe to cross. For further information contact Sweden's National Council for the Disabled: Statens Handikappråd, Liljeholmsvägen 30, Box 47611, S-11794; tel. (08) 681-05-61.

TRAVELLING to SWEDEN

Air: Scandinavia's flag carrier, SAS, most main European, and several North American airlines fly into Stockholm's Arlanda Airport. SAS, Braathen, and a few smaller operators offer internal connections to all parts of the country. Gothenburg's Landvetter and Malmö's Sturup airports have some international flights and also connections to the internal network.

Sea: From Britain, Scandinavian Seaways sails Harwich–Gothenburg throughout the year and Newcastle–Gothenburg in the summer. From Continental Europe, the main routes are Kiel–Gothenburg, Travemünde–Trelleborg or Travemünde–Malmö. From Denmark: Frederikshavn–Gothenburg, Helsingør–Helsingborg, Dragor–Malmö and Copenhagen–Malmö. The new Storebaelt (Green Belt) bridge will connect Copenhagen and Malö, Sweden when it is completed in 2000. It will provide access for both cars and trains.There are also services between Stockholm and Helsinki, Russia, and the Baltic States.

Rail: The main Continental cities are linked to Sweden by rail. From London (Victoria) either via Dover and Ostend, or from London

(Liverpool Street) via Harwich and Hook of Holland. From London it is also possible to travel (with your car) in *Le Shuttle* channel tunnel to France, from where you can continue your journey by road.

Alternatively, the Harwich–Esbjerg ferry or in summer the Newcastle–Esbjerg ferry (Scandinavian Seaways), connects with a train to Sweden via Copenhagen.

Coach: Many countries are connected to Sweden by coach. London to Stockholm, via Amsterdam, is cheap, but takes over 40 hours.

W

WATER

Sweden's water can be safely drunk from the tap, but Swedes also favour bottled water, and the local *Ramlösa* is on sale everywhere.

WEIGHTS and MEASURES (See also DRIVING)

Sweden uses the metric system. Weather temperatures are given in degrees Celsius (named after the Swede who invented the system).

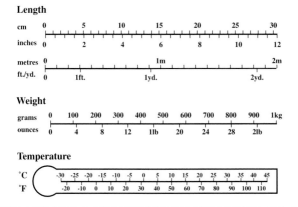

Sweden

WOMEN TRAVELLERS

Relationships between men and women in Sweden are probably the most "equal" in the world. There are many women's organizations, mostly connected to political parties, but two professional (rather than social) ones are:

Stiftelsen Kvinnoforum, Kungsgatan Stockholm; tel. (08) 20-08-00.

Yrkeskvinnors Riksförbund (Federation of Business and Professional Women), Drottninggatan 59 3tr, S-111-21 Stockholm, tel. (08) 10-74-14. It is affiliated to the International Federation of Business and Professional Women.

Y

YOUTH HOSTELS *(Vandrarhem)*

Sweden has 390 youth hostels (more than 100 open year-round) in a range of buildings from manor houses and former prisons (Långholmen in Stockholm) to purpose-built. Many lie in remote areas as well as towns and cater for all ages, with two- and four-bed rooms and family rooms. All have self-catering facilities, and some also serve meals.

Hostels are run by Svenska Turistföreningen (Swedish Tourist Club), who offer everything from camping packages or simple mountain cabins where you bring your own food, to hotel-standard accommodation, as well as operating small boat harbours and advising about cycling holidays and cycle hire.

Members of other countries' hostel associations qualify for cheap rates if they can produce their membership cards. The normal price is 70–125 Skr per night, plus 35 Skr for non-members. You should provide sheets or sheet sleeping bags but can also buy or hire them.

In summer, it's smart to book ahead, as this form of holiday is very popular. Further details and a list of hostels (price 80 Skr plus postage for youth hostel members, 95 Skr for non-members) is available from: STF, Box 25, S-101-20 Stockholm; tel. (08) 463-122-00, fax 678-1958. Details can also be found in the *International Youth Hostel Handbook*.

Recommended Hotels

Sweden has so many hotels in so many places that it is impossible to cover every area in full. Our list gives a selection in the three main cities, plus a few in more widespread areas. In the north in particular, except in towns, hotels may be far apart. In central and north Sweden many hotels and inns also have self-catering *stugor* for 2 to 6 people in their grounds. Hostel-style accommodation is not uncommon in the wilderness areas.

Hotels are of a high standard, but not cheap. MOMS (VAT) on hotels has, however, been reduced from 25% to 12%.

The price categories below are based on two people sharing a double room at full rates, including substantial cold-table breakfast, MOMS, and service charge.

❀❀❀	above 1,800 Skr
❀❀	1100–1,800 Skr
❀	below 1,100 Skr

STOCKHOLM

Anglais RESO Hotel ❀❀ *Humlegårdsgatan 23, S-10244 Stockholm; Tel. (08) 614-16-00, fax (08) 611-09-72.* Modern hotel opposite Humlegården Park. 212 rooms, including a number of comfortable cabins for hurried business travellers.

City Conference Hotel ❀❀ *Wallingatan 5, S-10724 Stockholm; Tel. (08) 506-16-00, fax (08) 791-50-50.* Comfortable hotel, quiet and well-planned, with an outdoor terrace.

City Hotel Gamla Stan ❀ *Lilla Nygatan 25, S-11028 Stockholm; Tel. (08) 24-44-50, fax (08) 723-72-51.* Occupying a 15th-century building at the Gamla Stan's south end. Unlicensed, popular with business and budget travellers. 51 rooms.

Sweden

Clas på Hornet ❀ *Surbrunnsgatan 20, S-11348 Stockholm; Tel. (08) 16-51-30, fax (08) 612-53-15.* Once an 18th-century inn, now a small hotel (10 rooms only) with lovely atmosphere. Situated in a quiet area, north of the centre.

First Hotel Reisen ❀❀ *Skeppsbron 12-14, S-11130 Stockholm; Tel. (08) 22-32-60, fax (08) 20-15-59.* Well-known 19th-century hotel on waterfront in Gamla Stan, with fine view towards Saltsjön. Good sauna. Piano bar. 114 rooms.

Grand Hotel ❀❀❀ *Blasieholmshammen 8, S-10383 Stockholm; Tel. (08) 679-35-00, fax (08) 611-86-86.* Luxury hotel overlooking water to Gamla Stan and the Royal Palace. Excellent restaurants. 321 rooms.

Hasselbacken Hotel ❀❀ *Hazeliusbacken 20, S-10055 Stockholm; Tel. (08) 670-50-00, fax (08) 663-84-10.* Mansion-style building grafted on to 19th-century timber restaurant. Views over Djurgården Royal Park. 111 rooms.

Hotell Diplomat ❀❀❀ *Strandvägen 7C, S-10440 Stockholm; Tel. (08) 663-58-00, fax (08) 783-66-34.* Waterfront hotel built in 1911 in Jugend style. View of boats at Nybroviken. 128 rooms.

Hotell Mälardrottningen ❀❀ *Riddarholmen, S-11128 Stockholm; Tel. (08) 24-36-00, fax (08) 24-36-76.* One of Stockholm's most unusual places to stay: a boat hotel in 1920s luxury yacht formerly owned by American millionairess Barbara Hutton. Situated in lovely anchorage at Riddarholmen. Gourmet restaurant (see page 142). 59 rooms.

Källhagens Wärdshus ❀❀ *Djurgårdbrunnsvägen 10, S-11527 Stockholm; Tel. (08) 665-03-00, fax (08) 665-03-99.* Classic modern building (1990) in the style of an 18th-century "Red House," in idyllic setting 2 km (1½ miles) from centre on Djurgårdsdviken (bay). Famed for its food. 20 rooms.

Långholmen ❉ *Gamla Kronohäktet, S-10272 Stockholm; Tel. (08) 668-05-00, fax (08) 720-85-75.* Unusual hotel in a former prison. On island, but convenient for the centre by car or public transport. Also offers Youth Hostel accommodation. 101 rooms.

Mornington Hotel ❉❉ *Nybrogatan 53, S-10244 Stockholm; Tel. (08) 663-12-40, fax (08) 662-21-79.* Central hotel, close to museums. English-style lobby bar and restaurant. 141 rooms.

Prize Hotel ❉ *Kungsbron 1, S-11122 Stockholm; Tel. (08) 14-94-50, fax (08) 14-98-48.* Next door to World Trade Centre, modern building (1989) with lots of glass. Breakfast hotel; popular with business travellers, but also a good family hotel. 158 rooms.

SAS Strand Hotel ❉❉❉ *Nybrokajen 9, Box 16396, S-10327 Stockholm; Tel. (08) 678-78-00, fax (08) 611-24-36.* Traditional building overlooking boats, with good view from its bar and restaurant on the top floor. 148 rooms.

Scandic Crown Hotel ❉❉ *Guldgränd 8, Box 15270, S-10465 Stockholm; Tel. (08) 51-73-53-00, fax (08) 51-73-53-11.* Above Slussen. Known for its restaurant, exclusive wine cellar, and original spirit shop from 1700. 319 rooms.

Sergel Plaza ❉❉ *Brunkebergstorg 9, Box 16411, S-10327 Stockholm; Tel. (08) 22-66-00, fax (08) 21-50-70.* On square set back from Hamngatan, in Stockholm centre. Lobby café and piano bar; good international restaurant. 406 rooms.

Stockholm Plaza ❉❉ *Birger Jarlsgatan 29, S-10328 Stockholm; Tel. (08) 56-62-20-00, fax (08) 56-62-20-20.* Unusual, stone-built 19th-century hotel with a pleasant atmosphere. Surrounded by shops and outdoor cafés; handy for centre and close to Humlegård Park. 155 rooms.

Victory Hotel ❉❉❉ *Lilla Nygatan 5, S-11128 Stockholm; Tel. (08) 14-30-90, fax (08) 20-21-77.* 17th-century building on a quiet street, close to Mälaren. Famous for its Lord Nelson memorabilia. Remains of the medieval city wall visible. 44 rooms.

AROUND STOCKHOLM

Grand Hotel Saltsjöbaden ✿✿ *S-13383 Saltsjöbaden; Tel. (08) 50-61-70-00, fax (08) 50-61-70-25.* Castle-style hotel set on the edge of Baggensfjärden. Good service and food. Swimming, sailing, tennis, fishing, and golf facilities available. 105 rooms.

Gripsholms Värdshus and Hotel ✿✿ *Kyrkogatan 1, S-64723 Mariefred; Tel. (0159) 247-250, fax (0159) 347-77.* Close to Mälaren and boat landing stage; good view of Gripsholm Slott. Sauna, gym, billiards, marked walking paths. 45 rooms.

Hotell Linné ✿✿ *Skolgatan 45, S-75002, Uppsala; Tel. (018) 10-20-00, fax (018) 13-75-97.* In the heart of Uppsala next to Linnéträdgården (Linné Gardens, the botanist's legacy: see page 36). Fine restaurant. Closed July. 117 rooms.

Hotell Svava ✿ *Bangårsgatan 24, Box 1425, S-75144 Uppsala; Tel. (018) 13-00-30, fax (018) 13-22-30.* New hotel, centrally situated and close to most sights. Well-equipped rooms plus an indoor shopping complex. 120 rooms.

Kohlswa Herrgård ✿ *S-73030 Kolsva, near Arboga; Tel. (0221) 509-00, fax (0221) 511-80.* 25 km (16 miles) north of Arboga, surrounded by its own parkland. Riding, fishing, shooting, tennis, golf, and walking. 44 rooms.

Sigtunastiftelsens Gästhem ✿ *Manfred Björkquists allé 2-4, S-19322 Sigtuna; Tel. (08) 592-589-00, fax (08) 592-589-99.* Located in woods near Mälaren. Cloister-like building with beautiful rose garden. 51 rooms.

Waxholms Hotell ✿ *Hamngatan 2, Box 63, S-18521 Vaxholm; Tel. (08) 541-301-50, fax (08) 541-313-76.* Comfortable, modest hotel set on Vaxholm island—ideal for watersports. 32 rooms.

MALMÖ

Garden Hotel ✿✿ *Baltzarsgatan 20, Box 4075, S-20311 Malmö; Tel. (040) 665-62-00, fax (040) 665-62-60.* Comfortable hotel with a beautiful lobby-lounge. Central location. 170 rooms.

Hotell Kramer ✿✿ *Stortorget 7, S-20221 Malmö; Tel. (040) 20-88-00, fax (040) 12-69-41.* Classic, turreted white building in Malmö's old main square. Good dining, nightclub. 107 rooms.

SAS Royal ✿✿ *Östergatan 10, S-21125 Malmö; Tel. (040) 23-92-00, fax (040) 611-28-40.* Half-timbered house with comfortable rooms. Restaurant claims best steak in Malmö. 224 rooms.

Scandic Concert House Hotel ✿✿ *Amiralsgatan 19, S-21127 Malmö; Tel. (040) 10-07-30, fax (040) 611-92-24.* Modern hotel in concert-hall building. Popular nightclub. 154 rooms.

THE SOUTH

Halltorps Gästgiveri ✿ *Högsrum, S-38792 Borgholm, Öland; Tel (0485) 850-00, fax (0485) 850-01.* 17th-century inn, 9 km (6 miles) from Borgholm on Öland. Superb restaurant. Swimming, riding, golf, and bird-watching. 36 rooms.

Karlelby Kro ✿ *S-27293 Tommarp, Skåne; Tel. (0414) 203-00, fax (0414) 204-73.* Charming white farmhouse 7 km (4 miles) west of Simrishamn, with a gourmet menu and fine wines. Pool, sauna, and gym. 21 rooms.

Örenäs Slott ✿✿ *S-26163 Glumslöv, Landskrona; Tel. (0418) 702-30, fax (0418) 731-81.* Stately building in park overlooking Öresund strait. Tennis and swimming. 126 rooms.

Provo Bis Star Hotel ✿✿ *Glimmervågen 5, Box 110-26, S-22011 Lund; Tel. (046) 211-20-00, fax (046) 211-50-00.* Seven minutes' walk from centre. Sauna, pool, and solarium, and close to golf, tennis, and badminton facilities, jogging track. 196 rooms.

Sweden

Slottshotellet—Romantik Hotel ✹✹ *Slottsvägen 7, S-39233 Kalmar; Tel. (0480) 882-60, fax (0480) 882-66.* View over Kalmarsund, and almost next to castle. Restaurant, bar, sauna and solarium. 45 rooms.

Strand Hotel ✹✹ *Strandgatan 34, S-62156 Visby, Gotland; Tel. (0498) 21-26-00, fax (0498) 27-81-11.* Modern hotel in Visby on Gotland island. Close to the shore and old city walls, as well as botanic gardens. Sauna and small indoor pool. 110 rooms.

GOTHENBURG

Hotell Eggers ✹✹ *Drottningtorget, S-40125 Göteborg; Tel. (031) 80-60-70, fax (031) 15-42-43.* Classic railway hotel, with marble floors, pillars, great chandeliers; Gothenburg's oldest, built in the mid-19th century. Close to Central Station, airport terminus and Nordstan shopping. 67 rooms.

Hotell Liseberg Heden ✹✹ *Sten Sturegatan, S-41138 Göteborg; Tel. (031) 750-69-00, fax (031) 750-69-30.* Set in Heden (heath). Pretty buildings in traditional style. Free ticket to nearby amusement park included. Good for families. 172 rooms.

Hotell Onyxen ✹ *Sten Sturegatan 23, S-41253 Göteborg; Tel. (031) 81-08-45, fax (031) 16-56-72.* Small breakfast hotel in elegant turn-of-the-century house. Family-owned. 34 rooms.

Hotell Opera ✹✹ *Norra Hamngatan 38, S-41106 Göteborg; Tel. (031) 80-50-80, fax (031) 80-58-17.* Located at Nordstan centre, close to Gustav Adolfs Torg. Free herring buffet for guests. Jacuzzi and sauna. 145 rooms.

Hotell Riverton ✹✹✹ *Stora Badhusgatan 26, S-41121 Göteborg; Tel. (031) 750-10-00, fax (031) 750-10-01.* Close to north harbour and the new Opera House. View of estuary from 11th-storey Sky Bar and Restaurant. Family-owned. 190 rooms.

Scandic Hotel Crown ✿✿✿ *Polhemsplatsen 3, S-41111 Göteborg; Tel. (031) 80-09-00, fax (031) 15-45-88.* Modern hotel with lovely atrium restaurant. Sauna, solarium, and gym. Family rooms available for two adults, two children. Close to Central Station and airport bus terminal. 320 rooms.

Scandic Hotel Rubinen ✿✿✿ *Kungsportavenyn 24, S-40014 Göteborg; Tel. (031) 81-08-00, fax (031) 16-75-86.* Occupies an excellent position on Avenyn, with the popular Restaurant Andra Våningen (see page 142) and Bistro. 191 rooms.

Spar Hotel Majorna ✿ *Karl Johansgatan 66-70, S-41455 Göteborg; Tel. (031) 42-00-20, fax (031) 42-63-83.* Cosy breakfast hotel near old Majorna harbour. Trams to the centre, sauna, free parking. Good rooms at budget price. 150 rooms.

THE WEST

Fregattan Comfort Hotel ✿✿ *Hamnplan, S-43244 Varberg; Tel. (0340) 677-00-00, fax (0340) 61-11-21.* In harbour square, with fine view of boats. Virtually on the bathing beach. Close to ferry to Grenå in Denmark. 95 rooms.

Hotell Alphyddan ✿ *Långatan 6, S-44030 Marstrand; Tel. (0303) 610-30/38, fax (0303) 612-00.* A few yards from a swimming pool and the famous little harbour in a town without cars; the gateway to Bohuslän's southern archipelago. 35 rooms.

Hotell Carl XII ✿ *Storgatan 41, S-66800 Dals-Ed; Tel. (0534) 611-55, fax (0534) 122-24.* Old hotel between two lakes, but close to centre of village. Bicycles and canoes for hire, sauna, and billiards. 38 rooms, plus hostel accommodation.

Ronnums Herrgård ✿ *S-46830 Vargön, near Vänersborg; Tel. (0521) 22-32-70, fax (0521) 22-06-60.* Superb Relais et Châteaux manor house in parkland south of Lake Vänern. Celebrated for its gourmet food, informality, and good service. Golf, tennis, watersports, and elk safaris arranged. 60 rooms.

Sweden

Sunds Herrgård ✿✿ *S-56028 Lekeryd near Jönköping; Tel. (036) 820-06, fax (036) 821-40.* Country house hotel on Lake Nåtarn. Good food and all comforts. Wildlife park, boating, fishing, riding, walking, and swimming. 65 rooms (including chalets).

Tanums Gestgifveri ✿ *S-45731 Tanumshede; Tel. (0525) 290-10, fax (0525) 295-71.* Charming 17th-century inn, well known for gourmet cuisine. Close to famous prehistoric carvings and beautiful fishing villages. Golf and fishing. 29 rooms.

Vadstena Klosterhotel ✿ *Klosterområdet, S-59230 Vadstena; Tel. (0143) 315-30/130-00, fax (0143) 136-48.* One of Sweden's oldest hotels in a 12th-century building. Next door to Skt Birgitta Kyrka on Lake Vättern, and five minutes' from Gustav Vasa's castle. Many original features. Restaurant. 29 rooms.

Värdshuset Hvitan ✿ *Storgatan 24, S-31121 Falkenberg; Tel. (0346) 820-90, fax (0346) 597-96.* A lovely 18th-century listed building in Falkenberg's old centre, with a garden leading down to the river. Close to sandy beaches. Golf and salmon fishing almost on the doorstep; sea sports. 35 rooms.

THE CENTRAL HEARTLAND

Fryksås Hotell ✿ *S-79498 Orsa; Tel. (0250) 460-20, fax (0250) 460-90.* Situated on high southern slopes above lakes Siljan and Orsasjön, with fine views over surrounding countryside. Within walking distance of Grönklitt Bear Park and a ski resort. Gourmet food and a strong musical tradition. Golf, tennis, fishing, and skiing. 13 rooms.

Green Hotel ✿-✿✿ *S-79370 Tällberg; Tel. (0247) 502-50, fax (0247) 501-30.* Rooms at different prices in various buildings with views of Lake Siljan, the oldest dating from the 16th century and housing many antiques and works of art. Waiters wear local costume. Both indoor and outdoor swimming pools. 101 rooms.

Hotel Åregården ✿ *S-83013 Åre; Tel. (0647) 178-00, fax (0647) 171-51.* Set in a charming turn-of-the-century hotel and ski lodge right in the centre of Åre. Sauna and good après-ski, as well as 4 restaurants, 2 nightclubs, and a disco. 170 rooms plus 280 in the ski lodge.

Hotell Södra Berget ✿ *Södra Stadsberget, Box 858, S-85124 Sundsvall; Tel. (060) 12-30-00, fax (060) 15-10-34.* Wonderful position at the top of Södra Berget, one of Sundsvall's two outlook hills, 3 km (2 miles) from the centre. Fabulous views, sauna, fitness room, slalom run, walking, and skiing. 182 rooms.

Hotel Tänndalen ✿ *S-84098 Tänndalen; Tel. (0) 684-220-20, fax (0) 684-224-24.* Family-run establishment situated in a popular all-year mountain resort area. Excellent food, wonderful mountain panorama, and indoor pool; golf, fishing, shooting, and canoeing available. Miles of ski tracks close by. 66 rooms.

Järvsöbaden Hotell ✿ *S-82040 Järvsö; Tel. (0) 651-404-01, fax (0) 651-417-37.* Rural hotel owned and run by the same family since it was built at the turn of the century. Situated on Öjeberget mountain, close to Järvsö Zoo on the outskirts of town. The grounds are lovely, and you can enjoy the tennis court, pool, fishing, and riding. 45 rooms.

Mjälloms Hotell ✿ *Hotellgatan 3, S-87031 Mjällom; Tel. (0) 613-211-14, fax (0) 613-214-75.* Occupies fantastic position on a point between two bays. Swimming (2 km/1½ miles to the beach), walking and jogging, fishing, golf, and a marina. *Smörgåsbord* with local specialities. 16 rooms.

RESO Hotel Örnsköldsvik ✿✿ *Lasarettsgatan 2, Box 10, S-89121 Örnsköldsvik; Tel. (0) 660-101-10, fax (0) 660-837-91.* Standard RESO hotel close to the centre and station and only a short walk away from the harbour, sea, and new "Paradisbadet" (fun pools). Restaurant, bar, and brasserie on the spot. 115 rooms.

Sweden

RESO Hotel Sundsvall ●● *Esplanaden 29, S-85236 Sundsvall; Tel. (0) 60-17-16-00, fax (0) 60-12-20-32.* Modern hotel in big red building, centrally located. Leisure centre with solarium, sauna, pool, jacuzzi, and bar. Restaurant, disco, piano bar and casino. 203 rooms.

RESO Hotel Winn ●● *Prästgatan 16, S-83131 Östersund; Tel. (0) 63-12-77-40, fax (0) 63-10-67-29.* Good RESO hotel in a central position on Stortorget, with a restaurant, cocktail bar, pool, and sauna. 177 rooms.

Scandic Hotel ● *Montörsbacken 4, S-82640 Söderhamn; Tel. (0) 270-180-20, fax (0) 270-189-01.* Well-furnished hotel with modern facilities. Restaurant and taverna-style fare. 87 rooms.

Ulfshyttans Herrgård ● *S-78196 Borlänge; Tel. (0) 243-513-00, fax (0) 243-511-11.* Old house with turret rooms and restaurant overlooking Lake Ulfssjön, plus library of old books and an art gallery. Ruined 18th-century blast-furnace (a reminder of Bergeslagen's iron-smelting days) on the grounds. 20 rooms.

Åkerblads Hotell och Gästgiveri ● *S-79370 Tällberg; Tel. (0) 247-508-00, fax (0) 247-506-52.* The Akerblad family have owned this building ever since the 1700s; it only became a hotel earlier this century. All built in solid timber with an old log cabin. Traditional bar, good home cooking. 89 rooms.

NORRLAND and the ARCTIC

Hotel Jokkmokk ●● *Solgatan 45, S-96040 Jokkmokk; Tel. (0) 971-553-20, fax (0) 971-556-25.* A good hotel in the heart of Sami country, with a restaurant that serves local specialities. Cocktail bar. Many activities, including helicopter transport to national parks, scooter safaris, and fishing instruction. 75 rooms.

Hotell Laponia ●● *Storgatan 45, S-93333 Arvidsjaur; Tel. (0) 960-108-80, fax (0) 960-104-89.* Comfortable modern hotel, close to Arvidsjaur's main lake. The restaurant serves Norrland specialities. There is a popular pub and disco and the hotel is a good base for rafting, walking, climbing, and skiing. 115 rooms.

Hotell Nordkalotten ✿ *Lulviksvägen 1, S-97254 Luleå; Tel. (0) 920-893-50, fax (0) 920-199-09.* Beautiful position on the heath, beside a small lake with cabins dotted among 800-year-old pines. Well located for outdoor activities: walking, cross-country skiing, and swimming. Indoor pool, sauna, and solarium; free loan of sports gear. 171 rooms.

Hotell Toppen ✿✿ *Blåvägen 238, S-92331 Storuman; Tel. (0) 951-117-00, fax (0) 951-121-57.* In a pine wood and handy for mountain walking and skiing; also very close to the railway station. Restaurant, pub, fishing, as well as a panoramic sauna with views over Storumansjön lake and mountain scenery. 63 rooms.

Jukkasjärvi Wärdshus and Hembygdsgård ✿ *S-98191 Jukkasjärvi; Tel. (0) 980-211-09, fax (0) 980-214-06.* Well-restored old timber building beside Torneälven river, 25 km (18 miles) from Kiruna. Hotel-standard *stugor* (cabins) plus more basic accommodation and local food. Good for outdoor activities. 45 four-bed *stugor.* (Runs the Arctic Hallen, ice hall, from January to May, see page 82.)

Lövånger Kyrkby ✿ *S-93010 Lövånger; Tel. (0) 913-103-95, fax (0) 913-107-59.* For a change, try this restored church village from the 15th century. Beautifully refurbished cottages, restaurant, leisure room, and sauna. 77 rooms.

Motell Björnen ✿ *Björnvägen 3, S-90640 Umeå; Tel. (0) 90-13-71-10, fax (0) 90-77-74-71.* Close to woodlands, 3 km (2 miles) from centre and 1 km (½ mile) from ski lift, with sauna, floodlit tracks, and bathing and fishing in Nydalssjön lake. 40 rooms.

Nya Dundret ✿✿✿ *Box 812, S-98221 Gällivare; Tel. (0) 970-145-60, fax (0) 970-148-27.* On lower plateau of Dundret, 4 km (3 miles) from the station; rooms, suites, and 90 *stugor* (cabins). Good base for skiing, fishing, guided walking tours. 125 rooms.

Prize Hotel ✿ *Rådhusplatsen 14, S-90328 Umeå; Tel. (0) 90-13-23-00, fax (0) 90-14-23-66.* Very central, modern hotel, with well-equipped rooms and facilities. Restaurant, cocktail and piano bars, grill, casino, sauna, and fitness room. 165 rooms.

RESO Hotel Ferrum ✿✿ *Lars Janssongatan 15, Box 22, S-98121 Kiruna; Tel. (0) 980-186-00, fax (0) 980-145-05.* Big, modern hotel near the station. Leisure centre, restaurant, cocktail bar, and casino. 170 rooms.

SAS Luleå ✿✿ *Storgatan 17, Box 267, S-95131 Luleå; Tel. (0) 920-940-00, fax (0) 920-882-22.* Central hotel, with modern rooms and indoor swimming pool, sauna, and health club. Restaurant, nightclub, and wine cellar. 198 rooms.

Silverhatten Hotell ✿✿ *Box 94, S-93090 Arjeplog; Tel. (0) 961-107-70, fax (0) 961-114-26.* Sitting on a mountain above town, with endless views. The restaurant combines good food (game, reindeer) with the panorama. 85 rooms.

STF Mountain Hotel Abisko ✿ *S-98024 Abisko; Tel. (0) 980-401-00, fax (0) 980-401-40.* A community in itself in Abisko National Park, close to where the train stops. Apart from the hotel, there are *stugor* (cabins) and hostel accommodation, a provisions shop, and a restaurant and bar in the hotel. Activities include boating, skiing, walking, mountain biking; guides and special guided "theme" weeks. 195 rooms.

Strand Hotel ✿✿ *Pite Havsbad, S-94128 Piteå; Tel. (0) 911-322-00, fax (0) 911-328-00.* Well-equipped rooms close to the harbour and bathing area, 10 km (7 miles) from the centre. Pool, sea fishing, boats for hire, and entertainment. 201 rooms.

Recommended Restaurants

Sweden offers a good range of restaurants in the main cities, but fewer in rural areas, where many of the best are in hotels (see hotel listings on pages 129–140). On a tight budget, make lunch, *dagens rätt* (see page 109), the main meal, and look out for offers such as Sunday specials. Tourist information publications such as *Stockholm This Week* give listings. Remember that some restaurants may be closed during July.

Eating out in Sweden can be expensive; the bill usually includes 21% *MOMS* (VAT) and service charge. It is customary to round up the bill to the nearest 10 Skr.

The establishments listed below offer both quality food and service, and represent good value for money. Prices are for an evening meal per person, without wine.

✿✿✿	above (sometimes well above) 250 Skr
✿✿	100–250 Skr
✿	below 100 Skr

STOCKHOLM

Blå Porten Café ✿ *Djurgårdsvägen 60; Tel. (0) 8-663-87-59/8-662-71-62.* Attractive restaurant in former art gallery, with central garden. Good, simple food, with emphasis on Swedish cuisine.

Centralens Restaurang ✿✿ *Central Station; Tel. (0) 8-20-20-49.* Set directly above the station hall, this restaurant offers good food; especially popular for breakfast. Simple dishes.

Hasselbacken ✿✿✿ *Hazeliusbacken 20; Tel. (0) 8-670-50-00.* Famous 19th-century restaurant with a large terrace garden. International and traditional Swedish food in a beautiful setting.

Hermans, The New Green Kitchen ✿ *Stora Nygatan 11; Tel. (0) 8-411-95-00.* Highly popular international vegetarian cooking. Its success has spawned a series of other locations throughout the city.

Leijontornet (Victory Hotel) ❋❋❋ *Lilla Nygatan 5; Tel. (0) 14-23-55.* High-class traditional Swedish cuisine in historic setting; glass floor over the ruins of medieval walls. (Closed July).

Mälardrottningen ❋❋❋ *Riddarholmen; Tel. (0) 8-24-36-00.* International and Swedish cuisine on Barbara Hutton's yacht.

Operakällaren ❋❋❋ *Operahuset; Tel. (0) 8-676-58-00.* A venerable institution (some 200 years old) with fine décor. Haute cuisine and home cooking. Famous for its *smörgåsbord*.

Stekhuset Falstaff ❋❋ *Tegeluddsvägen 90; Tel. (0) 8-663-48-40.* Excellent steakhouse; a view of the works in the open kitchen.

Victoria ❋❋ *Kungsträdgården; Tel. (0) 8-10-10-85.* Good traditional Swedish food overlooking Stockholm's popular garden square, with an outdoor verandah. Open late.

GOTHENBURG

Andra Vånigen ❋❋❋ *Hotell Rubinen, Kungsportsavenyn 24; Tel. (0) 31-81-08-80.* Chef Christer Svantesson provides gourmet food in his restaurant overlooking Avenyn.

Brassserie Ferdinand ❋❋ *Drottninggatan 41; Tel. (0) 31-10-71-60.* Good Swedish country cooking at reasonable prices.

Gamle Port ❋❋ *Östra Larmgatan 18; Tel. (0) 31-711-07-02.* Good international and Swedish food in 19th-century atmosphere.

The Place ❋❋❋ *Arkivgatan 7; Tel. (0) 31-16-03-33.* International cuisine in a small street close to Avenyn.

Restaurang Räkan ❋❋ *Loprensbergsgatan 16; Tel. (0) 31-16-98-39.* Food and fun: order shrimp and steer them across the "pool" in a radio-controlled mini-boat. Will delight children.

Restaurang Wärdshuset ✸✸ *Liseberg; Tel. (0) 31-83-62-77.* Good food in 19th-century atmosphere. Café, pub. Summer only.

Sjömagasinet ✸✸ *Klippan 6; Tel. (0) 31-24-65-10.* Seafood and Swedish specialities restaurant in an historic harbour warehouse built in 1775. Summer only (from 1 April).

MALMÖ

Centralens Restaurant ✸ *Central Station; Tel. (0) 40-766-80.* Station restaurant, sometimes with a troubadour in the evening. Snack bar and "dish of the day."

Kockska Krogen ✸✸✸ *Stortorget; Tel. (0) 40-730-20.* Swedish and international cooking in a vaulted 16th-century building.

Olgas ✸✸ *Pildammsparken; Tel. (0) 40-12-55-26.* Old inn set in Sweden's largest park. Simple, Swedish home-style food.

Rådhuskällaren ✸✸ *('Wein und Bierkeller') Kyrkogatan 6, Stortorget; Tel. (0) 40-790-20.* A 16th-century cellar restaurant, specializing in fish.

Restaurant Johan P ✸✸ *Saluhallen, Lilla Torg; Tel. (0) 40-97-18-18.* In Malmö's market hall; delicious fresh fish the speciality.

Restaurant Mongolian Barbecue ✸✸ *Södra Promenaden 23; Tel. (0) 46-23-00-26.* Meats spiced with sauces together with vegetables, cooked Mongolian style. Waiters are in costume.

Restaurant WB (Wein und Bierkeller) ✸ *Stortorget. Entrance: Kompanigatan 15; Tel. (0) 46-790-20.* Simple, mostly home cooking, such as *pyttipanna* (fried chopped meat, onion, and potato with beetroot, gherkin, and egg).

Översten ✸✸✸ *Kronprinsen, Regementsgatan 52; Tel. (0) 40-91-91-00.* Fine international cuisine and the city's best views across to Denmark from the 26th floor.

ABOUT BERLITZ

In 1878 Professor Maximilian Berlitz had a revolutionary idea about making language learning accessible and enjoyable. One hundred and twenty years later these same principles are still successfully at work.

For language instruction, translation and interpretation services, cross-cultural training, study abroad programs, and an array of publishing products and additional services, visit any one of our more than 350 Berlitz Centers in over 40 countries.

Please consult your local telephone directory for the Berlitz Center nearest you or visit our web site at http://www.berlitz.com.

Helping the World Communicate